STRATEGIES
FOR TEACHING
Middle-Level and
High School Guitar

MENC wishes to thank
Carolynn A. Lindeman, for developing and coordinating this series;
William E. Purse, James L. Jordan, and Nancy Marsters for
selecting, writing, and editing the strategies for this book;
Patricia Hackett for special editorial assistance;
and the following teachers for submitting strategies:

Martha Banghart	Patricia Hackett	Wanda I. Rivera-Ferri
Betty Benton	Romana Hartmetz	Sandra Rosengren
Dick Bozung	Kathleen Hubbard	Constance Ann Rybak
William A. Clark	Mary D. Jennings	Steven Schleicher
John Cochrane	Teresa Kane	Will Schmid
Robert A. Cutietta	Cynthia J. Kipker	Suzanne M. Shull
Robert E. D'Epiro	Ruth Kuhn	Rick Soens
Edward Duling	Ray Moyer	D. Charles Truitt
Marilyn M. Egan	Rick L. Orpen	Gregory H. Turner
Kenneth Eidson	David Park	Valerie Vander Mark
Ladonna Ellenberger	William D. Pere	Gregory L. Wallace
Cathy Ellis	Melissa E. Popovich	Mimi Watson
Mary Ann Fitzsimmons	Carlos Pozzi	Leo Welch
Charles Gary	Vincent Rahnfeld	Michael C. Zand
Grant Gustafson	Linda O. Rider	Steven T. Zvengrowski

STRATEGIES FOR TEACHING

Middle-Level and High School Guitar

Compiled and edited by
William E. Purse, James L. Jordan, and Nancy Marsters

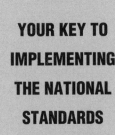

MUSIC EDUCATORS NATIONAL CONFERENCE

MENC MENC
MENC MENC

Series Editor: Carolynn A. Lindeman
Project Administrator: Margaret A. Senko

CONTENTS

PREFACE

The Music Educators National Conference (MENC) created the *Strategies for Teaching* series to help preservice and in-service music educators implement the K–12 National Standards for Music Education and the MENC Prekindergarten Standards. To address the many components of the school music curriculum, each book in the series focuses on a specific curricular area and a particular level. The result is eleven books spanning the K–12 areas of band, chorus, general music, strings/orchestra, guitar, keyboard, and specialized ensembles. A prekindergarten book and a guide for college music methods classes complete the series.

The purpose of the series is to seize the opportunity presented by the landmark education legislation of 1994. With the passage of the Goals 2000: Educate America Act, the arts were established for the first time in our country's history as a core, challenging subject in which all students need to demonstrate competence. Voluntary academic standards were called for in all nine of the identified core subjects—standards specifying what students need to know and be able to do when they exit grades 4, 8, and 12.

In music, content and achievement standards were drafted by an MENC task force. They were examined and commented on by music teachers across the country, and the task force reviewed their comments and refined the standards. While all students in grades K–8 are expected to meet the achievement standards specified for those levels, two levels of achievement—proficient and advanced—are designated for students in grades 9–12. Students who elect music courses for one to two years beyond grade 8 are expected to perform at the proficient level. Students who elect music courses for three to four years beyond grade 8 are expected to perform at the advanced level.

The music standards, together with the dance, theatre, and visual arts standards, were presented in final form—*National Standards for Arts Education*—to the U.S. Secretary of Education in March 1994. Recognizing the importance of early childhood education, MENC went beyond the K–12 standards and established content and achievement standards for the prekindergarten level as well, which are included in MENC's *The School Music Program: A New Vision.*

Now the challenge at hand is to implement the standards at the state and local levels. Implementation may require schools to expand the resources necessary to achieve the standards as specified in MENC's *Opportunity-to-Learn Standards for Music Instruction: Grades PreK–12.* Teachers will need to examine their curricula to determine if they lead to achievement of the standards. For many, the standards reflect exactly what has always been included in the school music curriculum—they represent best practice. For others, the standards may call for some curricular expansion.

To assist in the implementation process, this series offers teaching strategies illustrating how the music standards can be put into action in the music classroom. The strategies themselves do not suggest a curriculum. That, of course, is the responsibility of school districts and individual teachers. The strategies, however, are designed to help in curriculum development, lesson planning, and assessment of music learning.

The teaching strategies are based on the content and achievement standards specified in the *National Standards for Arts Education* (K–12) and *The School Music Program: A New Vision* (PreK–12). Although the strategies, like the standards, are designed primarily for four-year-olds, fourth graders, eighth graders, and high school seniors, many may be developmentally appropriate for students in other grades. Each strategy, a lesson appropriate for a portion of a class session or a complete class session, includes an objective (a clear statement of what the student will be able to do), a list of necessary materials, a description of what prior student learning and experiences are expected, a set of procedures, and the indicators of success. A follow-up section identifies ways learning may be expanded.

The *Guide for Music Methods Classes* contains strategies appropriate for preservice instructional settings in choral, instrumental, and general music methods classes. The teaching strategies in this guide relate to the other books in the series and reflect a variety of teaching/learning styles.

Bringing a series of thirteen books from vision to reality required tremendous commitment from many, many music educators—not to mention the tireless help of the MENC publications staff. Literally hundreds of music teachers across the country answered the call to participate in this project, the largest such participation in an MENC publishing endeavor. The contributions of these teachers and the books' editors are proudly presented in the various publications.

—*Carolynn A. Lindeman*
Series Editor

Carolynn A. Lindeman, professor of music at San Francisco State University and president of the Music Educators National Conference (1996–1998), served on the MENC task force that developed the music education standards. She is the author of three college textbooks (The Musical Classroom, PianoLab, and MusicLab) and numerous articles.

INTRODUCTION

Many years ago, as a soft-spoken Spaniard was elevating the acoustic guitar to a position of unprecedented importance and elegance, an out-of-work sign painter and sometime folk singer from Oklahoma proclaimed that the instrument had the ability to "kill Fascists." About the same time, a three-fingered Gypsy from France was crafting a body of work that would inspire generations. That these three individuals—Andrés Segovia, Woody Guthrie, and Django Reinhardt—all shared a passion for the same instrument is testament to the guitar's unique adaptability in the hands of a master. In this age of dizzying electronic advances, there is a major resurgence in the popularity of the "unplugged" guitar—further evidence that the guitar continues to provoke interest and inspiration.

The guitar's adaptability has made it one of the world's top-selling musical instruments. A novice on the instrument can quickly learn to produce a pleasant sound by strumming simple chords, but the guitar is a challenge to master. This dichotomy of simplicity and difficulty must be considered in forming any educational approach to the guitar.

There is no question about the important role the guitar plays in the field of contemporary music. It is a unique instrument in a portable package, combining unlimited harmonic, melodic, and rhythmic potential. In the hands of a music educator, the guitar offers tremendous flexibility as a solo, ensemble, or accompaniment instrument. A creative teacher can discover even greater applications. Though the guitar boasts a long history both in the United States and in other countries, development of curricular class guitar is a fairly recent phenomenon.

When MENC issued a call for guitar strategies, responses came from teachers eager to share their experiences and insights in using the guitar in the classroom. The editors are grateful to the many teachers who took the time and thought to share their successful classroom strategies. As a result of their efforts, *Strategies for Teaching Middle-Level and High School Guitar* provides a solid offering of skills and techniques that music educators have developed within their daily teaching practices. The strategies reflect the myriad styles, tastes, and interests of guitar educators nationwide and the creative ways that those interests are explored.

Strategies for Teaching Middle-Level and High School Guitar sets the stage for you, the educator, to learn about others' explorations and to develop your own applications. Like the other books in the series, this book will help you develop a personal and proactive approach to meeting the content and achievement standards in the National Standards for Music Education. We believe it is a good beginning, offering sufficient breadth to be helpful for all programs, regardless of size or scope.

Each strategy in this book includes a list of necessary materials. If a strategy requires a particular kind of guitar, or one guitar for a particular number of students, that is noted in the Materials. It is assumed that each student in a guitar class has a guitar and pick and that there is a piano or other keyboard instrument in the classroom.

Reveling in the guitar's diversity, the editors acknowledge Andrés Segovia, Woody Guthrie, and Django Reinhardt for their contributions. Special thanks to the Guitar Accessories Marketing Association (GAMA) and NAMM–The International Music Products Association for their support of the MENC/GAMA Guitar Task Force and guitar education in America's schools.

Given the wealth of ideas presented in this publication, developing a pedagogy to meet the Standards no longer seems such a daunting task. In fact, it seems quite an enjoyable one!

STRATEGIES
Grades 5–8

STANDARD 1A

Singing, alone and with others, a varied repertoire of music: Students sing accurately and with good breath control throughout their singing ranges, alone and in small and large ensembles.

Objective

- Students will sing a two-part composition accurately and with the breath control needed to support each phrase.

Materials

- "Bourrée for Bach," from *English Suite no. 2,* transcribed by Bennett Williams (Santa Barbara, CA: Sam Fox), SA or TB
- At least one guitar for each group of five students
- Snare drum with brushes or skin-covered hand drum (optional)
- Manuscript paper

Prior Knowledge and Experiences

- Students can play simple melodies on the guitar.
- Students can read treble- and bass-clef notation.
- Students have experience reading a simple vocal score with accidentals.
- Students have been introduced to breathing as indicated in a vocal score.

Procedures

1. Introduce students to scat singing by singing "la" and "du-bee," instead of lyrics, to the tune of a familiar song. Review the concepts of breathing at the end of phrases and of supporting entire phrases with proper breath control.

2. Teach students both parts in the first four measures of "Bourrée for Bach," telling them that they will be learning the rest of the piece on their own.

3. Divide the class into groups of five to allow for two students on each vocal part and one student on guitar. Ask the groups to learn to sing and play the piece, first by learning and polishing the vocal parts, then by learning to play at least one phrase of the bass line (scored for cello or string bass) on guitar. Have students transpose the guitar part an octave higher and write it out in treble clef on manuscript paper. Check their transpositions as students sing and play in their groups.

4. As the groups develop good ensemble skills, have them add a drum part with offbeat accents or lightly tap the top of the guitar.

5. Have each group demonstrate for the class as many phrases as it has learned. Ask the class to discuss the performances and identify which group sang most accurately and with the best breath control and ensemble skills.

6. Instruct students to return to their groups to work on areas that need improvement and to formulate a practice plan for subsequent sessions.

Indicators of Success

- Students sing "Bourrée for Bach" accurately and with the breath control needed to support each phrase.
- Students accompany their small ensembles with a bass part on guitar.

Follow-up

- In another Baroque selection—for example, "Bourrée in E minor," by Johann Sebastian Bach, in *Modern Approach to Classical Guitar,* Book 3, by Charles Duncan (Milwaukee: Hal Leonard Corporation, 1996)—have students learn to play the bass part and sing the upper line.

STANDARD 1B

Singing, alone and with others, a varied repertoire of music: Students sing with expression and technical accuracy a repertoire of vocal literature with a level of difficulty of 2, on a scale of 1 to 6, including some songs performed from memory.

Objective

- Students will sing a three-part composition with a level of difficulty of 2, observing various expressive markings.

Materials

- "The Black Snake Wind" (Pima Indian text), arr. Mary Goetze (New York: Boosey & Hawkes), SSA, Level 2
- Map of the United States
- Photographs or artifacts relating to Pima Indians

Prior Knowledge and Experiences

- Students can play simple melodies on the guitar.
- Students can read treble-clef notation.
- Students can read musical expression marks, including dynamic and tempo indications, fermatas, and tenuto marks.
- Students have sung simple melodies and have been rehearsing "The Black Snake Wind."

Procedures

1. Introduce students to Pima Indian culture by locating tribal areas on a U.S. map, exhibiting photographs or artifacts, and presenting information about the Pima tribe and the significance of the Black Snake Wind.

2. Explore with students the text of "The Black Snake Wind," guiding them to notice significant features of the music that relate to the text—for example, "twisting" is portrayed by running vocal parts.

3. Have students sing the three vocal lines of "The Black Snake Wind" without expression. Elicit students' suggestions for musical interpretation that would mirror the text. Instruct them to take special care in singing expressively, paying close attention to dynamic and tempo indications, fermatas, and tenuto marks.

4. Divide the class into groups of three with one student on each voice part. Have each ensemble practice singing the song expressively as a trio. Then guide trios in playing one or more phrases expressively.

5. Create a continuous performance of the entire composition by having separate trios of students sing and play consecutive sections of "The Black Snake Wind."

Indicators of Success

- Students sing and play "The Black Snake Wind" expressively.

Follow-up

- Have student trios each find a musical selection to develop creatively. Ask them to write the expressive markings in their music, practice singing and playing their selections, and perform them for the class.

STANDARD 1C

Singing, alone and with others, a varied repertoire of music: Students sing music representing diverse genres and cultures, with expression appropriate for the work being performed.

Objective

- Students will sing a song in Spanish with appropriate expression while accompanying themselves on guitar.

Materials

- "De colores," in *The Music Connection,* Grade 7 (Parsippany, NJ: Silver Burdett Ginn, 1997)

Prior Knowledge and Experiences

- Students have learned to play the C, F, and G7 chords.

- Students have been studying the history of the guitar and have been discovering the Spanish influence in the development of the guitar.

Procedures

1. Have students read the words of "De colores" in English and Spanish. Using any Spanish-speaking students as a resource, focus on the meaning of the Spanish words. [*Note:* The English translation closely parallels the Spanish text.]

2. Review the three chords used in "De colores" (C, F, and G7). Have students play the chords, one strum on the first beat of each measure, as you sing and play the song in English and then in Spanish.

3. Ask students to sing the melody using the letter names of the pitches. Then have them sing the words in English and Spanish (with or without playing). While working through any difficulties, promote expressive singing by helping students decide which words are key to the song's meaning. Have them sustain the longer notes for their appropriate duration.

4. Divide the class into groups of singers and players, and have the class rehearse the song in Spanish and evaluate song segments as needed, focusing on expression as well as technique. Guide them in singing some parts (or words) of the song louder than others, or introduce a crescendo or decrescendo. Have students exchange roles and perform the song again.

5. Ask all students to expressively sing and play the entire song together in Spanish.

Indicators of Success

- Students accurately sing and play "De colores" in Spanish with appropriate expression.

Follow-up

- Teach students the traditional harmony for "De colores," which is a third below the melody. Then have them sing the song in harmony a capella and while playing a guitar accompaniment.

(continued)

- Have students learn to sing and play songs such as the U.S. cowboy song "The Streets of Laredo," in *The Music Connection,* Grade 5 (Parsippany, NJ: Silver Burdett Ginn, 1995), and the Chilean cowboy song "My White Horse" ("Mi Caballo Blanco"), in *The Music Connection,* Grade 6; *Share the Music* (New York: Macmillan/McGraw-Hill, 1995), Grade 8; *Music and You* (New York: Macmillan/McGraw-Hill, 1991), Grade 8; or *World of Music* (Parsippany, NJ: Silver Burdett Ginn, 1991), Grade 7.

- Have students research and report on how cowboys in North America and Latin America sang and used the guitar.

STANDARD 1D

Singing, alone and with others, a varied repertoire of music: Students sing music written in two and three parts.

Objective

- Students will sing and play music in three parts in a guitar ensemble.

Materials

- "When the Saints Go Marching In," in *Guitar Ensemble,* Book 1, by Sandy Feldstein and Aaron Stang, Belwin's 21st-Century Guitar Library (Miami: CPP Belwin/ Warner Bros. Publications, 1994)

Prior Knowledge and Experiences

- Students have learned first-position notes in the key of C on the first three strings of the guitar.
- Students have sung simple guitar exercises using letter names of the notes, with and without guitar doubling.

Procedures

1. Divide the class into three groups and assign each group one of the three parts for "When the Saints Go Marching In." Have students learn to sing their assigned parts with letter names, using the guitar to find pitches.

2. Have each group sing its part, without guitars, for the other two groups, again using letter names. Ask listeners to critique the performances for correct pitches and rhythms.

3. When each group seems secure, combine the parts and have the class sing the song with words.

4. Ask all students to practice their parts in groups on their guitars.

5. When groups are secure on their guitar parts, have the class perform the piece as a three-part ensemble, with all students singing the words and playing their guitars.

Indicators of Success

- Students accurately sing and play a three-part arrangement of "When the Saints Go Marching In."

Follow-up

- Have all students learn to sing and play all three parts of "When the Saints Go Marching In." Then challenge students to play one part while singing another part.

Performing on instruments, alone and with others, a varied repertoire of music: Students perform on at least one instrument accurately and independently, alone and in small and large ensembles, with good posture, good playing position, and good breath, bow, or stick control.

Objective

- Students will play full G and C chords with bass notes in preparation for accompanying songs on their guitars.

Materials

- None required

Prior Knowledge and Experiences

- Students have been introduced to full fingerings for the G and C chords.

Procedures

1. Demonstrate, left hand alone, the chord change between the full G and C chords.

2. Have students play one measure of the G chord, using a slow, quarter-note strum in 4/4 meter. Ask them to move from the G to the C chord, coming to a full stop on the bass note of the C chord (fifth string, third fret). [*Note:* Only the bass note is fingered at the stopping point.] Make sure students use the third finger on the bass C. Repeat this procedure until they play the change smoothly and accurately.

3. Have students apply this same "stopping-on-the-bass-note" process to the change from the C chord to the G chord.

4. Ask students, as a class, to play one measure of each chord (G and C) using a slow, steady strum and pausing on each bass note as they change the chord. Have them carefully finger the rest of the chord as they make the change, before resuming the strum.

5. Continue the exercise, gradually reducing the time of each pause until students are able to change chords without a break in tempo.

Indicators of Success

- Students perform the chord changes between G and C, as an ensemble, with technical and rhythmic precision.

Follow-up

- Have students change chords with technical and rhythmic precision in two-chord songs in C major, such as "He's Got the Whole World in His Hands," "Ev'rybody Loves Saturday Night," and the Caribbean song "Marianne."

- With the above songs transposed to E major, have students use the "one-measure-at-a-time" method used in step 2 to play the E and B7 chords, which have the second finger in common.

Performing on instruments, alone and with others, a varied repertoire of music: Students perform on at least one instrument accurately and independently, alone and in small and large ensembles, with good posture, good playing position, and good breath, bow, or stick control.

Objective

- Students will perform a simple pentatonic melody with pitch and rhythmic accuracy and using proper fingering-hand position.

Materials

- "The Riddle Song," in *Modern Approach to Classical Guitar,* Book 1, by Charles Duncan (Milwaukee: Hal Leonard Corporation, 1996), or in *Hal Leonard Guitar Method,* Book 1, by Will Schmid (Milwaukee: Hal Leonard Corporation, 1995)

Prior Knowledge and Experiences

- Students have experience maintaining good posture and playing position.
- Students can identify and play the notes on the first four strings in first position on their guitars.

Procedures

1. Have students count out loud and clap the rhythm of the first phrase of "The Riddle Song."

2. Play the melody of the song while students follow the notation. Then play selected phrases and have students find them in their music.

3. Have students sing letter names in rhythm for the notes in the first phrase, visualizing where the notes would be played on the guitar. Point out that for the four strings used, only the E (on the fourth string), A (on the third string), and D (on the second string) are fingered.

4. Instruct students to play the notes of the first phrase twice, first while counting the beat aloud, then while singing the note names. Stress the importance of proper fingering-hand position, and help students make corrections as needed.

5. Have students repeat steps 3 and 4 for each remaining phrase of the song.

Indicators of Success

- Students perform "The Riddle Song" with pitch and rhythmic accuracy, using proper fingering-hand position.

Follow-up

- Have students independently use the method above to learn other melodies in G pentatonic, such as "Hills of Arirang," "Goodbye, Old Paint," and "Swing Low, Sweet Chariot." Then have individual students perform the melodies for the class, and ask the class to evaluate technical accuracy.

Performing on instruments, alone and with others, a varied repertoire of music: Students perform on at least one instrument accurately and independently, alone and in small and large ensembles, with good posture, good playing position, and good breath, bow, or stick control.

Objective

- Students will strum chords for a two-chord song, using correct body and hand position, keeping a steady beat, and singing.

Materials

- Notation or lead sheet for a familiar two-chord song in C major, such as "Ev'rybody Loves Saturday Night," "Hey Lidee," "This Old Man," or "Bingo."

Prior Knowledge and Experiences

- Students can keep a steady beat on classroom or other instruments.

Procedures

1. Introduce proper body and instrument position. Using the tempo of "Are You Sleeping?" (see step 4), have students pantomime strumming downward (not touching the strings), "playing" half notes at a steady beat. Help students maintain good position.

2. Distribute picks and show students how the pick is held. Have students pantomime as in step 1 and then strum a steady beat on the strings.

3. Introduce the simplified ("easy") G chord, with students holding the first string on fret three with the third finger. Check finger and wrist positions, and then have students strum only strings three (open), two (open), and one (third fret).

4. While students are rhythmically strumming the simplified G chord, begin singing "Are You Sleeping?" and invite students to join you. At some point, stop the group and have them begin playing the song together, perhaps adding a two-strum introduction.

5. Similarly introduce the simplified C chord, with students holding the second string on fret one and strumming strings three (open), two (first fret), and one (open). Have students sing and play "Row, Row, Row Your Boat" and "Three Blind Mice," using the simplified C chord. If the class includes students with changing voices who can do the singing, ask the class to practice playing the two songs in G major while students with changing voices sing.

6. Help students practice moving between the C and G chords, maintaining good body and hand position.

7. Review a familiar two-chord song in C major (see Materials). First, have students (silently) change chords and strum as you play and sing. Assist individuals as appropriate, and then have students play the chords. Have students both sing and play, demonstrating their knowledge of correct body and hand position.

Indicators of Success

- Students play simplified G and C chords with acceptable body and hand position.

- Students strum with precise rhythm while singing.

■ Students shift between G and C chords with precision.

Follow-up

■ Have pairs of students sing and play for one another, using correct body and hand position and steady-beat strumming. Ask students to tell their partners one good thing the partner did and one thing that needs improvement.

STANDARD 2C

Performing on instruments, alone and with others, a varied repertoire of music: Students perform music representing diverse genres and cultures, with expression appropriate for the work being performed.

Objective

- Students will perform a work song from Israel on the guitar, effectively expressing the sentiment of the song.

Materials

- "Zum Gali Gali," with accompanying CD, in *Share the Music,* Grade 5 (New York: Macmillan/McGraw-Hill, 1995); *The Music Connection,* Grade 5 (Parsippany, NJ: Silver Burdett Ginn, 1995); or *World of Music,* Grade 5 (Parsippany, NJ: Silver Burdett Ginn, 1991)
- Audio-playback equipment
- Audiocassette recorder, microphone, and blank tape

Prior Knowledge and Experiences

- Students can play the E-minor chord.
- Students can play the chorus of "Zum Gali Gali."

Procedures

1. Have students review playing the chorus of "Zum Gali Gali."

2. Ask students to read the English words for the song and decide what mood is expressed.

3. Play the recording of the song. Have students listen for and discuss how the song's mood is achieved through dynamics, accents, timbre of instruments, and so on.

4. Help students decide which expressive devices they will use in their performance of the song. Then have them sing and play the verses with expression.

5. Discuss with students whether the chorus should be played with the same or with different expression from the verses.

6. Have students sing and play the entire song as you tape the performance.

7. Play the tape and ask students to critique their performance, deciding whether and how well they carried out their ideas for an expressive performance.

Indicators of Success

- Students perform "Zum Gali Gali" with appropriate expression.
- Students identify elements of an expressive performance and critique a recording of their performance of "Zum Gali Gali."

Follow-up

- Have students perform previously learned music that requires expression similar to that used in their performance of "Zum Gali Gali." Then have them perform a familiar song that suggests contrasting expression—for example, "Michael, Row the Boat Ashore" or "When the Saints Go Marching In."
- Guide students in devising suitable contrasting interpretations of a song such as "He's Got the Whole World in His Hands."

STANDARD 2D

Performing on instruments, alone and with others, a varied repertoire of music: Students play by ear simple melodies on a melodic instrument and simple accompaniments on a harmonic instrument.

Objectives

- Students will identify chord changes by ear in a simple song and apply them in a guitar accompaniment.

Materials

- "New River Train," in *The Music Connection,* Grade 6 (Parsippany, NJ: Silver Burdett Ginn, 1995); or *World of Music,* Grade 6 (Parsippany, NJ: Silver Burdett Ginn, 1991)

Prior Knowledge and Experiences

- Students can play the D, G, and A7 chords.
- Students have had some experience identifying chord changes by ear.

Procedures

1. To review the D, G, and A7 chords, have students strum steady quarter notes in 2/4 meter, changing chords every two measures.

2. Sitting so that students cannot see your hands, sing and play "New River Train," telling students it is in the key of D major. Ask students to listen for how many different chords are used and to decide which chord ends the song.

3. Without singing, play the chord progression for students. Give students a few minutes to work out the chord progression on their own guitars. Replay the chords as necessary.

4. As you play and sing the song again, have students play along. For students having difficulty, help them relate the chord changes to the words of the song.

5. Have students accompany their singing of "New River Train."

Indicators of Success

- Students accompany their singing, changing to the correct chord at the correct time.

Follow-up

- Distribute sheets with words only to a familiar public-domain song that uses the I, IV, and V7 chords. Give students the final chord name and ask them to write the chord names for the rest of the song in the appropriate places.

- Introduce the ii and vi chords and have students aurally identify them in familiar melodies such as "We Shall Overcome" or "Morning Has Broken."

STANDARD 3A

Improvising melodies, variations, and accompaniments: Students improvise simple harmonic accompaniments.

Objective

- Students will improvise and embellish chord accompaniments by adding one finger to, or removing one finger from, a standard chord form.

Materials

- Songs such as "Battle Hymn of the Republic," "Buffalo Gals," or "She Wore a Yellow Ribbon," in *Mel Bay's Guitar Class Method,* vol. 1, by Mel Bay (Pacific, MO: Mel Bay, 1980); or other simple songs in D major from any book that teaches chord forms and strumming technique

Prior Knowledge and Experiences

- Students know the numbering of left-hand fingers and first-position chord forms for D major and A major.

- Students can strum first-position chords D major and A major with clarity and a sustained sound.

Procedures

1. Have students strum a D-major chord (strings 1–4 only) with clarity and a sustained sound (no muted sounds). Instructing them to keep all fingers down in position for the D-major chord, ask them to add the fourth finger to the first string at fret three and strum the new chord (Dsus4) with clarity and a sustained sound.

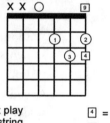

x = do not play
○ = open string
circled nos. = fingerings

4 = sus 4
9 = add 9

2. Ask students to strum a D-major chord once again. Then have them lift the second finger from the first string, creating another new chord (Dadd9). Have them strum the new chord.

3. Lead the class as they practice switching between the D, Dsus4, and Dadd9 chords, strumming each chord four times.

4. Follow the same procedure used in steps 1–2 with the A-major chord. Explain that by adding the note D to the chord (third fret, second string), an Asus4 results; and by lifting the third finger from the second string, an Aadd9 is formed. Repeat step 3 using these chords.

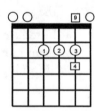

5. Using the selected simple songs in the key of D major (see Materials), have students, working individually or in groups, improvise and embellish chord accompaniments by using these new chords for selected D-major and A-major chords.

Indicators of Success

- Students improvise and embellish chord accompaniments to selected songs using the D- and A-major chords.

- Students add and remove fingers for the D- and A-major chords without stopping or losing the clarity and sustained sound of the chords.

Follow-up

- Encourage students to improvise accompaniments to songs they know. To expand their repertoire possibilities, extend the procedures above to the E-major chord, using the songs "Swing Low, Sweet Chariot" and "Sweet By and By," in Mel Bay's *Guitar Class Method,* vol. 1. Have students create Esus4 by adding finger 4 on string 3, fret 2 (A); and create Eadd9 by adding finger 4 on string 1, fret 2 (F#).

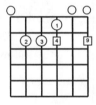

Improvising melodies, variations, and accompaniments: Students improvise short melodies, unaccompanied and over given rhythmic accompaniments, each in a consistent style, meter, and tonality.

Objective

- Students will improvise two-measure melody solo answers at the end of each phrase of a 12-bar blues in the key of E.

Materials

- "Rock Trax #1" and "Rock Trax #3," in *Rock Trax-1* by Will Schmid (Milwaukee: Hal Leonard Corporation, 1985), book and compact disc or audiocassette

- "Good Morning Blues," in *The Chord Strummer* by Will Schmid (Milwaukee: Hal Leonard Corporation, 1982), or in *Contemporary Class Guitar*, Book 1, by Will Schmid (Milwaukee: Hal Leonard Corporation, 1982)

- Audio-playback equipment

Prior Knowledge and Experiences

- Students can play melody notes E, F, and G on string 1 and B, C, and D on string 2 of their guitars.

Procedures

1. As students are entering the classroom, play "Rock Trax #3." Have students tune their guitars to the tuning notes at the beginning of the *Rock Trax-1* recording and warm up with other songs, chords, or melodies. Tell them that today they will begin learning to play one of the greatest African American styles of music—the 12-bar blues, which gets its name from its 12 measures, or "bars."

2. Have each student locate first-string notes E (open) and G (third fret) and briefly practice playing these two notes by themselves. Be sure students are using the third finger for the note G. Explain that they will practice playing all solos together by echoing what you play. Say: "I will play measures 1 and 2 (eight beats) like this":

Then say: "In measures 3 and 4, you echo on your guitar what I have just played. I will always start and end on the open E (first string). Try to play exactly what I play, using the same notes and rhythms. Later, you will have a chance to make up your own solos." After students have echoed the above example, play each of the following examples and have students echo them:

3. Repeat step 2 using second-string notes B (open) and D (3rd fret). Create patterns similar to those above and have students echo them.

4. Combine notes E and G on string 1 and B and D on string 2 (see example) for a two-measure teacher's "call," and have students echo. To make it easy for students to follow you, start and end each call on either the open E or open B. Be sure that students can see your left hand.

When students seem to have grasped the concept of echoing a call, repeat the process by having them play along with "Rock Trax #1," cut 2, in *Rock Trax-1*.

5. Have students turn to "Good Morning Blues" (12-bar blues in E) and learn to sing it with the background on "Rock Trax #3," cut 10, in *Rock Trax-1*. Ask students how many phrases the song has [three] and whether any of the phrases are almost the same as each other [first and second]. Show them how the phrases can be labeled "A A B."

6. Ask students to locate the two empty measures at the end of each phrase (measures 3–4, 7–8, 11–12) of "Good Morning Blues," and point out that the E chord is played in all of these measures. Tell students that they will learn the E chord later, but first they will be playing solos in the "open" measures, using just the notes E and G. Have the class sing "Good Morning Blues" and play the following solo in all of the open measures:

7. Have students sing and play along with "Rock Trax #3," singing each phrase with you and then improvising their own solos all at the same time in the open measures. Note that they should start and end on the note E. When students are successful in doing this, have them expand the scope of their solos by adding the notes B and D but still beginning and ending on E.

Indicators of Success

- Students improvise two-measure solos using the notes E, G, B, and D in measures 3–4, 7–8, and 11–12 of a 12-bar blues, beginning and ending their improvised solos within the prescribed measures.

Follow-up

- As students indicate that they are ready to improvise individual solos, have volunteers take turns while the rest of the class sings and supports them. Encourage students to create interesting syncopated rhythms, which are important to the style.

Improvising melodies, variations, and accompaniments: Students improvise short melodies, unaccompanied and over given rhythmic accompaniments, each in a consistent style, meter, and tonality.

Objective

- Students will improvise pentatonic melodies over single chords and over two- or three-chord progressions.

Materials

- Manuscript paper

Prior Knowledge and Experiences

- Students can perform simple melodies in first position, using quarter and eighth notes.

- Students have been introduced to the concept of free melodic improvisation.

- Students can play the G, C, D, Em, A, and Am chords with some fluency.

Procedures

1. Play a G-major pentatonic scale beginning on low D—D (string 4), E (string 4), G (string 3), A (string 3), B (string 2), D (string 2), E (string 1), G (string 1)—and have students practice it for a short period.

2. Have one group of students (rhythm guitars) keep a steady rhythm on a G chord while another group improvises freely using the pentatonic scale and steady quarter and half notes. [*Note:* Lead and rhythm guitarists should exchange roles periodically throughout this strategy.]

3. Ask the group that improvised in step 2 (lead guitars) which notes made suitable resting points, creating consonance, and which notes were passing or neighboring tones, creating dissonance.

4. Repeat steps 2 and 3 using C-major and D-major chords as the harmonic backgrounds. If some improvisers play C (from the C chord) and F# (from the D chord), help them understand that these notes are not part of the G-major pentatonic scale.

5. Have the group of rhythm guitarists, or individuals, play a repeating progression of G-C-D chords while the group of lead guitarists, or individuals, improvises as in step 4.

6. Repeat the process in steps 1–3 using the E-minor pentatonic scale, as follows: E (string 6), G (string 6), A (string 5), B (string 5), D (string 4), E (string 4), G (string 3), A (string 3), B (string 2), D (string 2), E (string 1), G (string 1). Assist students in identifying consonant and dissonant points in their improvisations.

7. Have rhythm guitarists play various combinations of the chords Em, A, and D, as lead guitarists improvise, still using the E-minor pentatonic scale.

Indicators of Success

- Students improvise G-major and E-minor pentatonic melodies freely over single chords and over two- and three-chord progressions.

- Students identify consonant and dissonant points in their playing.

Follow-up

- Have students compare pitches of the G-major and E-minor pentatonic scales and note their similarities and differences. Then have them improvise, alternating between the G-major and E-minor chords and identifying the shifts from major to minor.

- Divide class into duos and ask each duo to improvise and perform a short two-part composition that shifts between G-major and E-minor pentatonic.

STANDARD 4A

Composing and arranging music within specified guidelines: Students compose short pieces within specified guidelines, demonstrating how the elements of music are used to achieve unity and variety, tension and release, and balance.

Objective

- Students will compose phrases that exhibit balance and unity with given phrases.

Materials

- Chalkboard
- Manuscript paper
- Teacher-created, notated four-measure phrase (not ending on G), using pitches G, A, B, C, and D and note durations familiar to students

Prior Knowledge and Experiences

- Students can play and notate G, A, B, C, and D on strings two and three of the guitar.

Procedures

1. Have students review and play the pitches G, A, B, C, and D on strings two and three. Notate these pitches on the chalkboard with fingerings.

2. Notate the exemplary four-measure phrase on the chalkboard (see Materials). Have students tap the rhythm, name the pitches, and perform the phrase.

3. Distribute manuscript paper and have students notate the phrase. Then ask them to perform the phrase again.

4. Explain that they are going to compose a phrase and they need to "think like composers." Discuss with students the concept of unity (and variety) using examples at hand, such as students' clothing (repeating visual patterns) or the classroom (rows of light fixtures). Challenge students to discover what unifies the notated phrase, such as a repeating rhythm or pattern of pitches.

5. Play the phrase again, asking students to judge whether it sounds finished. Explain that the phrase is the first of a pair and that a second "answering" phrase that students will compose would provide balance. Briefly discuss the idea of a conversation in which one person's question is followed by a relevant answer.

6. Improvise a musically logical final phrase for the students, stopping just before the final tonic. Discuss the importance of the tonic, and replay the improvisation, ending on the tonic.

7. Have the class divide into pairs, and explain that they are to work cooperatively to compose and notate four-measure "answering" phrases that show unity (of pitches or rhythms) and balance with the given phrase and that end on the tonic. Remind them that they must be able to play their compositions. Circulate among the pairs to help them as needed. Then collect students' compositions, explaining that at their next meeting they will rehearse them and perform them for the class.

Indicators of Success

- Students compose answering phrases that have satisfactory balance and unity with given phrases.

- Students end their compositions on the tonic.

Follow-up

■ Have students perform their own compositions or those of their classmates. Guide them in evaluating the accuracy of their notation. Have the performers critique the compositions against the given criteria. Have students discuss, as a class, what was difficult about the composition assignment, commenting, for example, about whether it was easier to compose or to perform the pieces.

STANDARD 5A

Reading and notating music: Students read whole, half, quarter, eighth, sixteenth, and dotted notes and rests in 2/4, 3/4, 4/4, 6/8, 3/8, and alla breve meter signatures.

Objective

- Students will play a variety of rhythms in 4/4 meter from notation.

Materials

- Various rhythm cards with rhythmic notation for one measure in 4/4 meter
- Chalkboard
- Metronome (optional)

Prior Knowledge and Experiences

- Students can identify the numbers and letter names of the guitar strings.
- Students have played open strings using single-note durations, such as whole, half, and quarter notes.

Procedures

1. Have the class select a four-beat rhythmic pattern and then play each open string together, using picks, in that pattern.
2. Hold up one card with a familiar rhythm, and ask students to play each string using that rhythm.
3. Shuffle the cards, pull out a new one and hold it up, and have the class play the new rhythm on each string. Switch to a new card every four beats, using a metronome to keep the beat, if possible.
4. Repeat step 3, asking students to use either the thumb, index, or middle finger to pluck the open strings.
5. Challenge each student to play a rhythm from a card. Between solos, have the class repeat a selected rhythm.

Indicators of Success

- Students accurately play rhythms in 4/4 meter while looking at the rhythm cards.
- Students maintain a steady beat while playing rhythms from the cards.

Follow-up

- Have students use cards to practice reading rhythms and pitches, without looking at the left hand (or the guitar), as they learn fingered first-position pitches.

STANDARD 5C

Reading and notating music: Students identify and define standard notation symbols for pitch, rhythm, dynamics, tempo, articulation, and expression.

Objective

- Students will name, notate, and play sharps on the first six frets of the guitar.

Materials

- Chalkboard
- A die
- Manuscript paper

Prior Knowledge and Experiences

- Students can name, notate, and play the natural notes in first position on all six strings.

Procedures

1. Have students review the natural notes in first position by playing from notation on the chalkboard.

2. Introduce and explain any sharp, first by position and then by notation with the symbol. Have students name, play, and notate the sharp on manuscript paper.

3. Select a particular string and identify each pitch on the string chromatically, using sharp names. Write the fingering for each note on the chalkboard. [*Note:* Use the fourth finger for frets five and six.] Have students play the notes and copy the notation on manuscript paper.

4. Explain that students are going to write notes for the remaining five strings, using a game to do so.

5. Select a particular string and then roll the die to select a fret. Explain that one dot on the die will correspond to the first fret, two dots to the second fret, and so on. As each pitch comes up, have students name, play, and notate it.

6. Select a different string and proceed as in step 5, repeatedly, until first-position pitches on all strings are notated. [*Note:* Notes will not be in scale order.]

7. Have students name and play the pitches in chromatic scale order using sharps.

Indicators of Success

- Students correctly name, play, and notate natural and sharp first-position pitches on the first six frets of the guitar.

Follow-up

- Have students use two dice for the game used in the procedures—the first die to select a string and the second die to select a fret. Then have students work in groups of three—one person rolling the dice, one notating, and one playing.

- Explain that composers sometimes use random techniques, such as rolling dice, when composing. Have students experiment with using three dice to create aleatoric compositions.

STANDARD 6A

Listening to, analyzing, and describing music: Students describe specific music events in a given aural example, using appropriate terminology.

Objective

- Students will analyze, notate, and play on the guitar the chord progression of a given song.

Materials

- "I Love the Mountains," transposed to G major, with chords (G, Em, Am, D) in *Share the Music,* Grade 4 (New York: Macmillan/ McGraw-Hill, 1995); *Music and You,* Grade 4 (New York: Macmillan/McGraw-Hill, 1991); or *World of Music,* Grade 4 (Parsippany, NJ: Silver Burdett Ginn, 1991)
- Chalkboard
- Manuscript paper

Prior Knowledge and Experiences

- Students can sing "I Love the Mountains" by rote and have not seen the notation.
- Students can identify the tonal center of "I Love the Mountains."
- Students can identify the letter names of the guitar strings.
- Students can spell major and minor chords using notation or guitar fret numbers.

Procedures

1. Give students the starting pitch, in G major, and ask them to sing "I Love the Mountains," pausing after each phrase to sing the tonal center. Have students repeat the exercise, calling it the "Tonal Challenge Game." Encourage students to maintain the tonal center and not go sharp or flat. Ask them to check their accuracy by playing the G string on a guitar.

2. Lead students to discover which two-measure phrases can be sung in harmony [all four phrases]. Have them play the Tonal Challenge Game while singing the song in a two-, three-, or four-part canon, each group entering two measures after the previous group.

3. On the chalkboard, notate the pitches (G-B-D) of the first chord. Briefly review the construction of major and minor chords. Ask students to determine how to play the pitches together on the guitar. Have them play the pitches together each time the G chord is indicated.

4. Ask students to locate the Em, Am, and D chords in the transposed score. Have them spell and then notate each chord on manuscript paper. As they complete this task, have them play the chords on their guitars.

5. Have students locate the Em chord in the first phrase of the transposed score, and ask them to decide which of the chord tones is used in the melody [the root]. Similarly, have them locate and identify the Am chord root in the melody. Challenge students to decide what happens to the melody on the first use of the D chord [the third of the chord is used]. Be sure that students use proper terminology when discussing tonal center, chord progressions, and so on.

6. Have students sing "I Love the Mountains" in unison while playing the accompanying chord progression and listening for how the melody notes relate to the chords.

Indicators of Success

- Students sing the song and maintain its tonal center.
- Students analyze, notate, and play the chords of the song.
- Students use appropriate terminology in their analysis of the song.

Follow-up

- To review chord tones, divide the class into three groups and assign each group to sing (on "loo" or "doo") and play one part (root, third, or fifth) of the chords for "I Love the Mountains." Point out common tones between the chords and have students sing the chords in tempo. Then, asking some students to sing the melody, have students play their assigned parts on guitar to accompany the singing.

- Have students use their knowledge of repeated chord progressions to explore the repetition in musical forms such as the canon—for example, Canon in D major by Johann Pachelbel or various pop songs.

STANDARD 7B

Evaluating music and music performances: Students evaluate the quality and effectiveness of their own and others' performances, compositions, arrangements, and improvisations by applying specific criteria appropriate for the style of the music and offer constructive suggestions for improvement.

Objective

- Students will compare and contrast the effectiveness of three performances—two commercially recorded versions and a recording of their own performance of a folk song.

Materials

- Copies of student- and teacher-generated list of criteria for performance evaluation
- Lyrics and chords for "Goodnight Irene," by Huddie Ledbetter and John A. Lomax, in *A Tribute to Woody Guthrie & Leadbelly*, student text and teacher's guide, by Will Schmid (Reston, VA: Music Educators National Conference [MENC], 1991)
- Audio recording of *Folkways: A Vision Shared*, Columbia 44034 (available from MENC)
- Videotape of *Folkways: A Vision Shared* (New York: CBS Music Video Enterprises, 1988; available from MENC)
- Audio-playback equipment, including audiocassette recorder, microphone, and blank tape
- Videocassette recorder and monitor
- Chalkboard or blank transparency
- Overhead projector, if transparency is used

Procedures

1. Introduce the song "Goodnight Irene," choosing a key that employs chords students already know. [*Note:* The song uses only I, IV, and V chords.] Teach students the song, in 3/4 meter, having them use a "thumb-brush-brush" accompaniment pattern.

2. When students are comfortable with the chord changes, record the class performance, inviting students to sing as you lead them so that they can concentrate on their playing. Play the recording and encourage students to listen critically and quietly.

3. Show the Willie Nelson performance of the song on the videotape *Folkways: A Vision Shared.* Have students identify the meter and form. Then help them determine the key of the song by listening and by watching Nelson's fingers on his guitar. Repeat the process with the Brian Wilson performance of the song on the audio recording of *Folkways: A Vision Shared.*

4. Help students create a chart on the chalkboard (or a transparency) that compares the form, key, and meter of the three versions—Nelson's, Wilson's, and their own. Also, distribute the copies of the evaluative criteria and have students use the criteria as they decide to what extent each performance produced the expected or intended effect, considering each performance's intended style (such as folk, blues, country, or pop). Have students look and listen for special ways of playing and singing, such as picking, strumming, or producing rhythm effects on the guitar; or rasp, slides, or slurred words in the voices. Ask them to decide how the performers introduced contrast (or lacked contrast) in the dynamics, tempo, and timbre of voice and instrument.

5. Ask students to consider their evaluation of their own performance and identify ways they could improve their version by incorporating ideas contained in the other two versions. If they decide to change the meter to 4/4, as Brian Wilson did, help them devise an appropriate accompaniment pattern.

6. Record the students as they perform their new version of the song. Have them listen to both their new and original recordings and then discuss whether the effectiveness of their performance improved as a result of the lesson.

Prior Knowledge and Experiences

- Students can accompany simple three-chord songs on the guitar.

- Students can identify the form, meter, and key of simple songs using correct terminology.

- Students have discussed the emotional intent and impact of particular songs.

Indicators of Success

- Students evaluate their own performance of "Goodnight Irene" and those of Wilson and Nelson, using criteria from the list developed previously.

- Students compare and contrast the three performances.

- Students make suggestions for improving their own performance based on their evaluations.

- Students improve the effectiveness of their own performance by incorporating suggestions from their evaluations.

Follow-up

- Play Leadbelly's original recording of "Goodnight Irene," from the audio recording *Folkways: The Original Vision,* Smithsonian/ Folkways SF-40001 (available from MENC), and the Weavers' 1950s version, on *The Weavers' Greatest Hits,* Vanguard Twofer VCD-15/16. Ask students to compare these recordings with the Nelson and Wilson versions and the class recording.

STANDARD 8B

Understanding relationships between music, the other arts, and disciplines outside the arts: Students describe ways in which the principles and subject matter of other disciplines taught in the school are interrelated with those of music.

Objective

- Students will describe similarities between the history, society, and music of African Americans and Jamaicans of African ancestry.

Materials

- "Reggae Feet," three-part, in *Explore It! Guitar and Style,* by Nancy Marsters (Tallahassee, FL: Class Guitar Resources, 1992)

- Recording of "One Love," performed by Bob Marley and the Wailers, on *Legend,* Tuff Gong/Island 422-846210

- Recording of "Oh, Happy Day," performed by the Edwin Hawkins Singers, on *Oh, Happy Day,* BMG Special Records 7243-8-56442-2-1

- Map that includes the USA, the Caribbean, and West Africa

- Audio-playback equipment

- Chalkboard

Procedures

1. Play the recording of "One Love." Have students clap along on the offbeats and identify the country and the type of music [Jamaica; reggae]. Then have students locate Jamaica on the map.

2. Play the recording of "Oh, Happy Day," having students similarly clap and identify [USA; African American gospel]. Help them discover and list on the chalkboard musical similarities between the two songs [displaced accents, strict meter and tempo, natural vocal style, call-and-response form, improvisation—African influence; harmony, instruments, form—European influence]. Establish that both pieces were created by people of African ancestry. Replay music as appropriate.

3. Review with students the distinctive back-beat rhythm of reggae, assigning students to the melody, rhythm, or bass parts of "Reggae Feet," which they have previously learned.

4. Write on the chalkboard Jamaica's national motto: "Out of many, one people." Discuss how this applies to the multicultural populations of both Jamaica and the United States, and mention that the two countries also have some similar history and culture. Have students name some ethnic groups living in each country [Jamaica—peoples from Africa, Spain, India, Nepal, China, Syria]. Help them decide how these different groups arrived in each country: by force (slaves), by choice (immigrants), or by birth (native peoples).

5. To demonstrate ethnic origins, have all class members stand. Say, "If one of your parents came to America from another country, please sit down." Then, "If one of your grandparents came to America from another country, please sit down." Continue until only one or two students remain standing. Have students verbalize the purpose (and result) of this demonstration.

6. Explore how, in both the United States and Jamaica, Africans were sold into slavery, and throughout their ordeal, they struggled to retain their culture and maintain social cohesion. Use the map to show patterns of European exploration and the primary West African areas from which slaves were transported. Have students decide what newcomers might have brought with them, even if they had no material possessions [social customs, arts, language].

Prior Knowledge and Experiences

- Students have experience analyzing rhythm, form, and vocal timbre of music that they have heard.

- Students have performed the distinctive "back-beat" rhythm of reggae.

- Students have learned to play the three parts of "Reggae Feet."

7. Conclude by discussing, and listing on the chalkboard, how music functions in people's lives: for rites of passage (birth, death, marriage), entertainment (work, socializing), institutions (religious, educational, political), and so on.

Indicators of Success

- Students describe musical characteristics of African derivation.

- Students describe similarities between the historical, social, and musical cultures of Jamaica and the United States.

Follow-up

- Have students demonstrate reggae back beat in body movement (dance).

- Ask students to share their recreational listening experiences (MTV, recordings) in class, describing pieces in terms of the African musical influence they hear.

- Have students research and report on the lives and times of, and musical influences upon, African American composers such as Louis Morceau Gottschalk, W. C. Handy, and Duke Ellington.

STANDARD 9A

Understanding music in relation to history and culture: Students describe distinguishing characteristics of representative music genres and styles from a variety of cultures.

Objective

- Students will describe the purpose of an Israeli folk song in modern Israel, sing and accompany the song on the guitar, and identify its distinguishing characteristics.

Materials

- "Tzena, Tzena," transposed to the key of A, in *The Music Connection,* Grade 5 (Parsippany, NJ: Silver Burdett Ginn, 1995); *Share the Music,* Grade 5 (New York: Macmillan/McGraw-Hill, 1995); or *Music and You,* Grade 6 (New York: Macmillan/McGraw-Hill, 1991)

- Repeating chord rhythm for "Tzena, Tzena" on the chalkboard or a transparency (see step 1)

- Overhead projector, if transparency is used

Prior Knowledge and Experiences

- Students can play the repeating chord progression (I, IV, V7, I) of "Tzena, Tzena" (see step 1) with a simple, rhythmic strum, but they have not yet learned the song.

Procedures

1. Have students review the repeating chord pattern for "Tzena, Tzena":

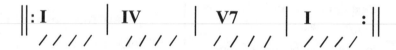

2. With students referring to the chord rhythm for "Tzena, Tzena," invite them to play chords while you sing and play the song. Review with students what the song is about [text varies depending on source] and where it originated [Israel].

3. To demonstrate a line dance, have three or four students form a line, placing their hands on their neighbors' shoulders. As you sing "Tzena, Tzena," instruct the group to move to the left, using rhythmic "step-together" footwork. Emphasize the cooperation necessary for this dance, and help students speculate how this relates to aspects of Israeli culture, such as the kibbutz (communal farming settlements). [*Note:* See Follow-up for sources for the hora dance.]

4. Have class reassemble. Discover what students know about Israel and Israeli music. Help them in understanding that the people of Israel come from many different homelands—such as Eastern Europe, Russia, Spain, Africa, and India—with different folk songs. Explain that, therefore, musicians have created modern folk songs (and dances) to help unify the people and to create a tradition especially for Israel. Note that there are some common characteristics in Israeli music, even though various cultural components (Eastern European, Middle Eastern, and North African) have merged to form what we know as Israeli music.

5. Guide students in describing characteristics of "Tzena, Tzena," including the simple repetitive form, use of syncopation, and dotted rhythms. Explain that these are characteristics of Israeli music, particularly in folk dance. Ask what the meter is, and explain that duple meter is common in Israeli folk music. Also explain that the guitar—like the accordion, drums, or flute—is commonly used to accompany such music.

6. Introduce the words of "Tzena, Tzena," with students softly singing as you sing and play. Have students practice pronouncing "Tzena" ("Zay-nuh"). Discuss and clarify words and pitches as appropriate. Refine students' singing by focusing on each of the song's three parts until they are secure. Have them sing and play the entire song.

7. Review what students have learned about Israel and about the people and folk music of modern Israel.

Indicators of Success

- Students perform "Tzena, Tzena" with acceptable pitch, words, chords, and tempo.

- Students describe the origins and purposes of Israeli folk music.

- Students describe distinguishing characteristics of Israeli folk music.

Follow-up

- Have students sing "Tzena, Tzena" as a three-part round, asking some students on each part to play the chord rhythm they have learned. Then have the class speculate how this multipart singing fits into what they know about Israel.

- Have students dance the hora with coordinated footwork and an acceptable tempo. [*Note*: Dance directions for the hora are included in *The Music Connection*, Grade 5 (teacher edition); *Share the Music*, Grade 5; and *Music and You*, Grade 6.] Ask some students to accompany the dancing by playing the chord rhythm they have learned for "Tzena, Tzena" on the guitar.

STRATEGIES
Grades 9–12

STANDARD 1B

Singing, alone and with others, a varied repertoire of music: *Students sing music written in four parts, with and without accompaniment.*

Objective

- Students will sing and play a four-part Renaissance composition with a stylistically appropriate, student-created guitar accompaniment.

Materials

- "What If I Never Speed," by John Dowland, transcribed by Peter Warlock, SATB, Level 4, in *Five Centuries of Choral Music for Mixed Voices,* Book 1 (Milwaukee: Hal Leonard Corporation, 1941)

- Recording of "What If I Never Speed," on *Ayers and Lute Lessons,* performed by countertenor and period-instrument consort, Musique d'Abord/Harmonia Mundi HMA CD-1901076

- Audio-playback equipment

Prior Knowledge and Experiences

- Students can read a four-part choral score that includes treble- and bass-clef notation.

- Students have experience singing in four-part harmony.

- Students can play simple melodies on the guitar.

Procedures

1. Teach students the SATB parts of "What If I Never Speed."

2. When students have learned their parts, divide the class into quartets. Have each quartet practice the piece in four parts on the guitars.

3. Play the recording of the lute and voice performance of "What If I Never Speed," asking students to determine how the voices and the lute relate [homophonic with some embellishment]. [*Note:* Sixteenth-century vocal and instrumental versions of Dowland's songs rarely differed much, and the singers often accompanied themselves.] Have the class devise a stylistically appropriate interlude, coda, or introduction.

4. Have students sing "What If I Never Speed" with and without guitar accompaniment throughout, working toward coordinated pitch, rhythm, and expression (timbre, dynamics, tempo). Help them evaluate whether their performance is stylistically appropriate.

Indicators of Success

- Students sing "What If I Never Speed" in four parts.

- Students create and perform a stylistically appropriate vocal and guitar arrangement of the composition.

Follow-up

- Have students trace the history of the lute and guitar, discovering how they have been used in different eras to accompany the voice.

- Have students note the date of "What If I Never Speed" (1603), and ask them to research the life and times of the composer John Dowland (England, 1563?–1626).

STANDARD 1C

Singing, alone and with others, a varied repertoire of music: Students demonstrate well-developed ensemble skills.

Objective

- Students will sing a four-part choral arrangement, playing a guitar accompaniment and demonstrating ensemble skills such as dynamic balance, rhythmic cohesiveness, and tonal unity.

Materials

- "Mister Sandman," by Pat Ballard, arr. Ed Lojeski (Milwaukee: Hal Leonard Corporation), SATB, Level 4

Prior Knowledge and Experiences

- Students can read a four-part choral score that includes treble- and bass-clef notation.
- Students have experience singing in four-part harmony.
- Students can play simple melodies on the guitar.

Procedures

1. Beginning with a discussion of the sound of cascading water in nature, discuss "sound cascades" (descending sustained-note arpeggios) in music. Explore the cumulative addition of sounds by asking some students to sing and sustain a pitch while others add and sustain pitches above or below the original pitch.

2. On their guitars, have students practice the four-part sustained arpeggios in the "Mister Sandman" introduction. Help students to dampen the strings carefully and decide what timbre, tempo, and dynamics are appropriate.

3. Have students play the arpeggios again, singing while they are playing.

4. Assign students to sing the four vocal parts of "Mister Sandman" according to their voice range. Rehearse parts in large or small groups until all parts are secure.

5. Continue rehearsing the piece, having students focus on ensemble skills, such as dynamic balance, rhythmic cohesiveness, and tonal unity.

6. Ask students to locate other "filler parts"—vocal interludes, written as "bum" in the score—that use cascading arpeggios. Have them sing the filler parts on the syllable "bum" and play them on their guitars. After students have practiced the filler parts on guitar, have them sing the entire piece, with piano accompaniment, some students playing the introductory cascades and other filler parts on guitars. Encourage students to give particular attention to ensemble skills.

Indicators of Success

- Students sing "Mister Sandman" in four parts with guitar accompaniment, performing pitches and rhythms accurately.
- Students demonstrate their ensemble skills by achieving dynamic balance, rhythmic cohesiveness, and tonal unity.

Follow-up

- Have students rehearse "Mister Sandman" in vocal quartets. Then have each quartet perform for the class.

STANDARD 1E

Singing, alone and with others, a varied repertoire of music: Students sing music
written in more than four parts.

Objective

■ Students will read, sing, and play on guitars a four-part antiphonal Renaissance madrigal.

Materials

■ "Echo Song" by Orlando di Lasso, double chorus of mixed voices, Level 4, in *Five Centuries of Choral Music for Mixed Voices,* Book 1 (Milwaukee: Hal Leonard Corporation, 1941)

Prior Knowledge and Experiences

■ Students can read a four-part choral score that includes treble- and bass-clef notation.

■ Students have experience singing in four-part harmony.

■ Students can play simple melodies on the guitar.

■ Students have notated a song such as "Frère Jacques" using augmented note values.

Procedures

1. Review the idea of "echo" by having students sing in canon "Frère Jacques" or another familiar song in which the parts enter at two- or four-beat intervals. Also review 4/2 meter.

2. Divide class into four parts and have them learn to sing the SATB lines of "Echo Song." Then have them learn to play their own vocal lines on guitar.

3. Challenge students to perform their parts in two different ways: guitar with voice echo, and voice with guitar echo. Once they are secure in their parts, have the class perform the song first with guitars in four parts and then with voices in four parts.

4. Have students sing "Echo Song" as originally composed for double antiphonal chorus.

Indicators of Success

■ Students sing and play "Echo Song" with accurate pitches and rhythms.

■ Students maintain melodic and rhythmic cohesiveness when singing and playing "Echo Song" in three different arrangements—guitars in four parts, voices in four parts, and voices in eight parts.

Follow-up

■ Have students research the life and times of the composer Orlando di Lasso (Belgium, 1532–1594).

■ Have students compare—either performing or using recordings and scores—the polyphonic style of madrigals by di Lasso with a song of John Dowland (see strategy 1B, grades 9–12) in which the melodic interest lies chiefly in the top line.

STANDARD 2B

Performing on instruments, alone and with others, a varied repertoire of music: Students perform an appropriate part in an ensemble, demonstrating well-developed ensemble skills.

Objective

- Students will perform a three-part folk song arrangement with attention to ensemble skills they identify and evaluate, including uniform phrasing, pitch accuracy, blend, balance, and rhythmic cohesiveness.

Materials

- "Scarborough Fair," in *Complete Guide for the Guitar,* by Cathy Ellis (Miami: Ellis Family Music, 1990); or a similar guitar ensemble arrangement with at least three parts
- Selected works students have studied previously (see step 1)
- Chalkboard
- Videocamera and blank videotape; or audiocassette recorder, microphone, and blank tape
- Videocassette recorder and monitor (if videocamera is used)

Prior Knowledge and Experiences

- Students have learned their assigned parts for "Scarborough Fair."

Procedures

1. Review phrasing and dynamics from music students have studied previously. Discuss with students and elicit examples of how modifying these elements can make music more expressive. Guide students in determining what other factors affect expression, such as pitch accuracy, blend, balance, rhythmic cohesiveness, and uniform phrasing. Write terms on the chalkboard as students discuss and discover examples.

2. Divide the class into groups of two or three on the same part, according to their assigned parts for "Scarborough Fair." Have them tune their guitars to a standard pitch and then rehearse their parts, focusing on the factors listed in step 1.

3. Have the groups perform for the class one at a time. Involve the class in evaluating each performance, challenging them to offer specific (and positive) suggestions for improvement.

4. Reorganize the class into quartets or sextets, with all parts represented in each group. Have students retune their instruments and rehearse "Scarborough Fair" in parts. Ask them to keep in mind previous evaluations and discussions. Circulate among the groups and confer with each, eliciting from students an evaluation of their ongoing rehearsal and their plans for improvement.

5. Bring students together for a large-group audiotaped or videotaped performance. After taping, show students the tape and discuss with them the strengths and weaknesses of their rendition. Tape additional takes as time allows until, by consensus, students are satisfied that their performance meets most of their criteria.

Indicators of Success

- Students perform a three-part arrangement of "Scarborough Fair" with uniform phrasing, pitch accuracy, blend, balance, and rhythmic cohesiveness.
- Students establish suitable criteria for evaluating their performance and accurately evaluate their performance.

Follow-up

- Have students sing and play "Scarborough Fair," using the same expressive elements in singing and playing.

- Teach students the conducting pattern for "Scarborough Fair," and have them take turns conducting small ensembles or the entire class. Encourage student conductors to strive for an expressive rendition.

STANDARD 2C

Performing on instruments, alone and with others, a varied repertoire of music: Students perform in small ensembles with one student on a part.

Objective

- Students will perform a four-part chorale on their guitars, using a sequencer and MIDI file to learn their parts.

Materials

- *Bach Chorale Standard MIDI Files* (Pacific, MO: Mel Bay), IBM (95050IMD); Macintosh (95050MMD)

- *Mel Bay Presents Bach Chorales for Guitar* by Bill Purse (Pacific, MO: Mel Bay, 1994), solo, duet, trio, or quartet

- Sequencer (either hardware- or software-based)

Prior Knowledge and Experiences

- Students can read and play simple melodies on the guitar.

Procedures

1. Demonstrate the operation of the sequencer to the entire class. Show them how to load and play back the standard MIDI files from *Bach Chorale Standard MIDI Files.*

2. Assign students one part in different chorales, from *Mel Bay Presents Bach Chorales for Guitar,* to practice with the sequencer. [*Note:* Each chorale in the text has multiple arrangements (quartet, trio, duet, solo).] Have advanced students work on the more difficult soprano lines. [*Note:* Soprano players may need help reading ledger lines.]

3. Demonstrate how the sequencer's tempo can be regulated and how a person can play a duet with the sequencer by muting and unmuting selected tracks. Discuss with students the purposes and musical advantages of these features, and have students practice accessing them.

4. Determine a schedule for students' use of the available equipment, and establish time limits. Also, explain what they will do while waiting to use the equipment.

5. When students are secure with their parts, divide the class into quartets with one student on a part. Have quartets take turns practicing with the sequencer.

6. Have each ensemble perform its chorale for the class, with and without the sequencer. Encourage some students to conduct their ensembles.

Indicators of Success

- Students perform their parts in a Bach chorale with acceptable rhythm, pitch, and tempo, both with and without the aid of a sequencer.

Follow-up

- With one student on a part, have students sightread Bach chorales in *Mel Bay Presents Bach Chorales for Guitar,* with or without a sequencer.

Advanced

STANDARD 2D

Performing on instruments, alone and with others, a varied repertoire of music: Students perform with expression and technical accuracy a large and varied repertoire of instrumental literature with a level of difficulty of 5, on a scale of 1 to 6.

Objective

■ Students will expressively play a selected solo guitar study with a level of difficulty of 5, giving the outer voices greater prominence than the inner parts.

Materials

■ Study in A, op. 60, no. 3, by Matteo Carcassi (any standard edition)

Prior Knowledge and Experiences

■ Students have well-developed arpeggio technique.

■ Students have thorough knowledge of the fingerboard.

■ Students have begun practicing Carcassi's Study in A.

Procedures

1. Have students play through Carcassi's Study in A, sounding only the first note of each triplet and leaving out the arpeggiated chords (see block intervals in step 3) of the inner voices, as follows:

measures 1–3, treble and bass only

2. Ask students to describe the relationship between the treble and bass voices. [They create a dialogue with each other.]

3. Reintroduce the inner voices, but have students play them as block intervals on the second half of the beat, rather than as arpeggiated triplets, as follows:

measures 1–3, inner voices blocked

4. Ask students which of the parts should be more prominent. [The outer voices.] Have students perform with exaggerated balance, making the outer voices loud and the inner voices especially soft.

5. Have students play the piece as written (with the chords arpeggiated), maintaining balance among the voices.

Indicators of Success

■ Students perform Carcassi's Study in A with good balance among the voices, bringing out the dialogue between the treble and bass parts.

Follow-up

■ To help students develop a deeper understanding of solo guitar music, have them similarly analyze and perform classical guitar works of a polyphonic nature, such as "Spanish Ballad," traditional (any standard edition), or "Moderato," in C major, by Mauro Giuliani (any standard edition).

STANDARD 3A

Improvising melodies, variations, and accompaniments: Students improvise
stylistically appropriate harmonizing parts.

Objective

- Students will improvise a chord-based accompaniment for a given melody, demonstrating an understanding of how the underlying chords relate to the melody, and incorporate "borrowed" chords in their harmonizations.

Materials

- Recording of "Rocky Mountain High" by John Denver, on *Rocky Mountain High,* RCA 5190-2-R
- Audio-playback equipment
- Any simple, familiar melody in D major, with quadruple meter, clearly defined phrases, and some long note values—for example, "Michael, Row the Boat Ashore," in *Get America Singing . . . Again!,* compiled by Music Educators National Conference (Milwaukee: Hal Leonard Corporation, 1996); or "Bye, Bye Blackbird" or "Top of the World," in *The Melody Book: 300 Selections from the World of Music for Piano, Guitar, Autoharp, Recorder and Voice,* 3d ed., by Patricia Hackett (Upper Saddle River, NJ: Prentice-Hall, 1998)

Procedures

1. Play the recording of "Rocky Mountain High," asking students to notice when they hear expected chords and when they hear unexpected ones. [In the verses, an F-major chord harmonizes the note A, where a D-major chord would be expected.] Help students realize that both the F-major and D-major chords contain A, and either chord could be used. Explain that the F-major chord is a "borrowed" chord. Tell them that they are going to improvise chords for a song, using both types of chords.

2. Pair the students and distribute the selected melody. Assign one of each pair to play or sing the melody, and ask the other student in each pair to accompany.

3. Ask students to improvise a simple chordal accompaniment using the I-IV-V7 chords in D major. Have them change chords at regular two-, four-, or eight-beat intervals.

4. When all pairs have completed step 3, direct their attention to a place in the melody that has a long note. Have students find substitute chord(s) for the melody note in question, as in step 1.

5. Review with students more examples of borrowed chords. Have students reharmonize a standard V-I cadence in the selected song. For example, the key of D melody notes C# to D are normally harmonized by A major and D major. Instead, have them try an F# chord for the pitch A and a B♭ chord for the pitch D. Discuss with them how this works, and have them play the cadence both ways.

6. Give partners time to complete their harmonizations, and have them take turns playing (or singing) the melody and playing the improvised chordal accompaniment for the class.

Indicators of Success

- Students improvise chordal harmonizations for a given melody.
- Students use borrowed chords to harmonize the melody.

Follow-up

- To give students practice in finding new chords, have them name at least five chords above a given a tonic key note, at least three of which are borrowed from another key.

Prior Knowledge and Experiences

- Students know the spelling of common major and minor triads and dominant seventh chords.

- Students can analyze the relationships of I, ii, IV, V, and vi chords in a given key.

Improvising melodies, variations, and accompaniments: Students improvise stylistically appropriate harmonizing parts.

Objective

- Students will improvise a standard blues accompaniment using open strings and barre chords.

Materials

- Selected studies in simple A blues form (V in measures 9 and 10; I in measures 11 and 12), such as "Muted Blues," "The Jack Flash Riff," or "Hard Rock Blues," in *Guitar Rock Shop,* Book 1, by Aaron Stang, Belwin's 21st-Century Guitar Library (Miami: CPP Belwin/Warner Bros. Publications, 1994)
- Metronome or drum machine

Prior Knowledge and Experiences

- Students have experience playing barre chords across three strings.
- Students can play simple "bass-strum" style.
- Students can play arpeggios using a pick or their fingers.
- Students have studied the basic blues progression and have listened to blues recordings.

Procedures

1. Have students play through the blues progression using selected studies in simple A blues form.

2. Explain to students the importance of the *turnaround*—the last four measures in the blues, which bring you back (or turn you around) to the first measure.

3. Review with students the chords in the basic blues progression. Have them memorize the "telephone number" for the blues progression with a new turnaround (422-1111) and the order of corresponding chord changes in the key of A. [*Note:* Numbers represent the number of measures in 4/4 meter that each chord will sound (four measures of A, two measures of D, and so on).]

4	2	2	1	1	1	1
‖: A	D	A	E	D	A	E :‖

4. Have students use the one-measure "riffs" from the studies in step 1 to create the new turnaround in the telephone number for the blues (E5 [root + fifth], measure 9; D5, measure 10; A5, measure 11; E5, measure 12).

5. Review three-string barre forms for the A, D, and E chords.

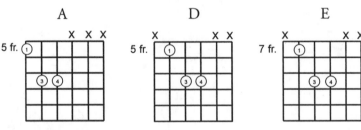

x = do not play
circled nos. = fingerings

6. Set a metronome or a drum machine to a moderate tempo, and have students apply the blues telephone number to the bass pattern and chords. Ask them to repeat the progression several times. Encourage experimentation with the rhythms and, if they are able, the chord voicings. Suggest that they experiment sliding up to a barre chord from one fret below, which works well with pairs of barre chords. Or have them experiment with playing eighth-note triplet rhythms (12/8 feeling) with the three-string barre chords.

7. Have selected individuals, playing solo or with you, demonstrate for the class their improvisations over the blues progression with the new turnaround.

Indicators of Success

- Students improvise accompaniments using open strings and barre chords within the framework of the blues chord progression.

- Students change barre chords at the appropriate times while keeping a steady tempo.

- Students describe the importance of the turnaround in the blues progression.

Follow-up

- Have students use barre chords to improvise a blues in the key of E or the key of C.

- Play recorded examples of advanced turnarounds used by jazz artists playing 16-bar blues—for example, "Lady Bird," by Tadd Dameron, on *The Smithsonian Collection of Classic Jazz,* vol. 3, Smithsonian Collection of Classic Jazz RD 033-3.

STANDARD 3B

Improvising melodies, variations, and accompaniments: Students improvise rhythmic and melodic variations on given pentatonic melodies and melodies in major and minor keys.

Objective

- Students will improvise variations on a given melody over a rhythm and blues accompaniment using major and minor pentatonic scale patterns.

Materials

- "Rhythm and Blues," in *Guitar Today,* Book 1, by Jerry Snyder (Van Nuys, CA: Alfred Publishing Company, 1982)

- Chalkboard, or transparencies, with guitar tablature for E-minor and E-major pentatonic scales (see figure), and with examples showing construction of major and minor scales

- Overhead projector, if transparencies are used

Prior Knowledge and Experiences

- Students can read and perform simple melodies using first-position pitches.

Procedures

1. Have students play through the accompaniment for "Rhythm and Blues" a few times.

2. Demonstrate the solo melody of "Rhythm and Blues" as it would be played in third position (measures 9–12 should be played in first position), and have students play along until they perfect it.

3. Explain the construction of major and minor pentatonic scales and display examples on the chalkboard or from a transparency. Then display guitar tablature for E-major and E-minor pentatonic scales (see figure). Have students play up and down the scales in third position several times, using a variety of rhythm patterns.

4. Divide the class into two groups. Have one group play the accompaniment for "Rhythm and Blues," repeating the twelve measures eight or more times, while the other group plays the written solo. Beginning with the second chorus, have the solo group improvise variations on the given melody, using the pentatonic scales in third position.

5. Repeat step 4, having the groups switch roles.

6. Have students explore several performance variations, such as the following:

   - accompanists and soloists switching parts every two measures; or

   - solo groups playing two-measure individual improvisations or "trading eights" (playing eight-measure solos in turn).

7. Have several students improvise on the second chorus at the same time in different ranges of the guitar while other students play the accompaniment.

Indicators of Success

- Students improvise variations, in E-major and E-minor pentatonic, on the given melody.

Follow-up

- Have students use barre chords to improvise on pentatonic scales, transposing the 12-bar blues progression to other keys—for example, G, A, B♭, and C.

- Have students listen to and analyze the blues guitar improvisations of guitarists such as B. B. King or Eric Clapton.

E-minor Pentatonic

E-major Pentatonic

Numbers = fingerings

STANDARD 3B

Improvising melodies, variations, and accompaniments: *Students improvise rhythmic and melodic variations on given pentatonic melodies and melodies in major and minor keys.*

Objective

- Students will improvise on the melody of a song that moves from a minor key to its related major key.

Materials

- Recording of "El Condor Pasa" ("If I Could"), on *Simon and Garfunkel's Greatest Hits,* Columbia Records CK-31350
- Audio-playback equipment

Prior Knowledge and Experiences

- Students have experience with basic bass, lead, and rhythm guitar techniques, including the concepts of rhythmic and melodic variation.
- Students can identify the names of the strings and the notes on the fingerboard in the first position.
- Students can play the E-minor and G-major scales.
- Students have experience constructing major scales on manuscript paper.

Procedures

1. Play the recording of "El Condor Pasa," asking students to listen to the lyrics and the form of the song. Note that the lyrics concern choices, and point out that there are musical choices to be made when improvising.

2. Discuss the concept of relative major and minor scales. Explain that each key signature can be used for a major scale or a relative minor scale starting on the sixth degree of the major scale.

3. Explain the rubato introduction (Em–Am–Em) and section A, which uses G and Em chords. Divide the class into groups for lead, rhythm, and bass guitar parts.

4. Being sure that students' guitars are tuned to the recording, teach section A to each group, as follows:

   Lead guitars: Play the first phrase of the melody as written, and note how the pitches are drawn from the natural E-minor scale. When the phrase repeats, use rhythmic and melodic variations, and try to make each successive repeat increasingly more complex in its variation of the melody.

   Rhythm guitars: Improvise rhythmic strums on the G and Em chords.

   Bass guitars: Improvise a rhythm on the roots of the chords—E (open sixth string) and G (sixth string, third fret).

5. Have students play with the recording, improvising on section A, listening to section B, and playing on section A.

6. Teach students section B, in G major, which uses three chords (C, G, and Em). Ask students to name the one pitch common to these three chords (G). Then have them improvise on these chords, as they did with the G and Em chords for section A in step 3, lead guitars improvising on the melody using the G-major scale; rhythm guitars improvising rhythmic strums on all three chords; and bass guitars improvising a rhythm on the roots of the three chords. Play the recording again, having students improvise in sections A and B.

7. Repeat steps 4–6 as needed, having students switch parts so that everyone has the opportunity to play lead guitar and improvise on the melody.

Indicators of Success

- Students improvise variations on the melody of "El Condor Pasa," using the E-minor and G-major scales.

- Students improvise rhythmic patterns on the chord roots in "El Condor Pasa."

- Students demonstrate an understanding of the chord progressions and show rhythmic and melodic creativity in their improvisations.

Follow-up

- Have students sing and play Daniel Almonica Robles's original version of "El Condor Pasa," in *The Melody Book: 300 Selections from the World of Music for Piano, Guitar, Autoharp, Recorder and Voice*, 3d ed., by Patricia Hackett (Upper Saddle River, NJ: Prentice-Hall, 1998). Ask them to analyze the melodic and rhythmic figures in the notation. Then have them review melodic and rhythmic devices that can be incorporated into an improvisation, such as the following: melodic devices—neighboring tones, passing tones, turns, arpeggios, acciaccaturas, appoggiaturas; rhythmic devices—dividing a quarter note into smaller parts, reversing notes in a dotted figure, syncopation.

- Ask each student to prepare a melodic improvisation that incorporates melodic and rhythmic devices they have identified. Have each student perform his or her improvisation while other class members sing and play a simple chordal accompaniment. Ask class members to discuss, compare, and evaluate each improvisation.

STANDARD 3C

Improvising melodies, variations, and accompaniments: *Students improvise original melodies over given chord progressions, each in a consistent style, meter, and tonality.*

Objective

- Students will improvise a melody over a given chord progression.

Materials

- Poster displaying the poem "Good and Clever" by Elizabeth Wordsworth (see figure); or another four-line poem or poem with four-line verses

Prior Knowledge and Experiences

- Students can play simple chord progressions and accompany themselves on the guitar as they sing melodies.

Procedures

1. Have students practice a given four-measure chord progression until they can play it accurately.

2. Ask students to read the poem "Good and Clever" in rhythm as they strum the progression.

3. Ask students to sing three-pitch arpeggios of each chord as they play the progression again (humming or singing "doo").

4. Have students use primarily chord tones and explore a melody, humming or singing "doo," that complements the rhythm of the poem.

5. Give students time to work individually or in groups to develop their songs, adding the poem's words and a strumming pattern.

6. Have students perform their improvisations twice, consecutively, to be sure they are singing what they have planned.

Indicators of Success

- Students improvise a melody that fits the chord progression and the rhythm of the poem.

Follow-up

- Have students improvise a melody over a given chord progression, using poetry, meter, and mode that contrast with those in the procedures above.

Good and Clever

If all the good people were clever,
And all clever people were good,
The world would be nicer than ever
We thought that it possibly could.

But somehow 'tis seldom or never
The two hit it off as they should,
The good are so harsh to the clever,
The clever, so rude to the good!

So friends, let it be our endeavour
To make each by each understood;
For few can be good, like the clever,
Or clever, so well as the good.

—*Elizabeth Wordsworth*

Improvising melodies, variations, and accompaniments: *Students improvise original melodies over given chord progressions, each in a consistent style, meter, and tonality.*

Objective

- Students will improvise a melody, based on the pentatonic scale, over a blues progression in the key of A minor.

Materials

- Handout illustrating the A-minor, D-minor, and E-minor pentatonic scales (see step 2)

- Recordings of a blues guitar solo, such as a performance by B. B. King, Buddy Guy, or Robben Ford

- Audio-playback equipment

Prior Knowledge and Experiences

- Students have played a 12-bar blues in A minor using straight and shuffle rhythms, the "boogie" pattern, and palm muting.

- Students have studied the "turnaround" (transition) between verses in a blues song.

- Students have studied the A minor pentatonic scale and used it as a basis for improvisation.

Procedures

1. Review with students the blues progression in A minor using the "boogie" pattern, both straight and shuffle eighth notes, and palm muting. Also review the turnaround.

2. Distribute the handout and review the A-minor, D-minor, and E-minor pentatonic scales.

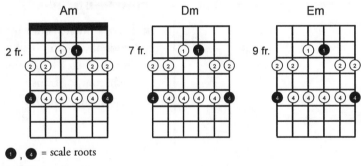

●, ④ = scale roots

circled nos. = fingerings

Note: This is a movable pentatonic form.

3. As you play the blues progression, have students take turns soloing. Encourage all efforts by telling students that "for now, there are no wrong notes." Expect some students to confine themselves to a scale or patterns while others move outside the given scale.

4. Play a recording of a blues guitar solo, asking students to listen for the solo versus rhythm parts, improvisation, strums, turnaround, and so on.

5. Give students time to improve their own improvisations based on what they have heard. Divide the class into duos or trios and have one student in each ensemble play the solo as the others play the rhythm part. [*Note:* The playing will be continuous if the players switch roles during each turnaround.]

6. Reassemble the class members and have individual students play solos while others play the rhythm part. Encourage students to verbalize what they are doing and how their performances may have improved after hearing a blues guitarist and practicing more.

(continued)

Indicators of Success

- Students improvise solos based on pentatonic scales over a blues progression in A minor.
- Students correctly play the chord changes and play in tempo.

Follow-up

- Have students work independently or in pairs to compose blues lyrics after learning about blues lyrics and form. Help students fit the lyrics to a blues chord progression, create a melody, and notate their compositions in a lead-sheet format. Then have students record their compositions or perform them for the class.

STANDARD 4B

Composing and arranging music within specified guidelines: Students arrange pieces for voices or instruments other than those for which the pieces were written in ways that preserve or enhance the expressive effect of the music.

Objective

- Students will arrange an accompaniment to a folk song, preserving or reinterpreting the song's original intent.

Materials

- Collections of folk songs [*Note:* Avoid choosing songs that must be transposed because the chords may be too difficult for students.]

- Recordings of the selected music (optional)

- Audio-playback equipment, if recordings are used

- Manuscript paper

Prior Knowledge and Experiences

- Students can play first-position major, major-seventh, minor, minor-seventh, and dominant-seventh chords and their barre-chord counterparts.

- Students can play several beginning- to intermediate-level accompaniment patterns.

- Students can compose and notate simple melodies using conventional music notation.

- Students can notate chord progressions using "slash" notation.

Procedures

1. Explain to the class that they are going to create a new accompaniment for a familiar song. Briefly discuss the reasons for creating an arrangement different from the original.

2. Present a number of folk songs to the class and help them arrive at a consensus about which five or six songs to use. Have each student select one of the songs. If recordings are available, play and discuss the styles they hear in the five or six selected songs.

3. Have students, working individually or in groups, develop scratch lead sheets for their songs. Explain that they should write the treble clef and key signature, lyrics under the staff, measure bars, slashes for beats in each measure, guitar chord symbols above the slashes, and metronomic marking.

4. Review with students the chords of each of the five or six songs. Help students simplify any chords that are too complex for them.

5. Ask students to choose accompaniment styles for their songs that meet these two criteria: (1) they can play the accompaniment acceptably; and (2) the new accompaniment either preserves the original style of the song or a given recording of it or creates a new interpretation of the song. Explain that they might explore accompaniment styles such as the Carter-style strum, Travis-style fingerpicking, thumb-brush strum with alternating bass, and reggae strum, or they might create an original strum.

6. Have students write final copies of their lead sheets, including an indication of the chosen style, as well as the title, composer, lyricist, and copyright information.

7. With the class singing, have each student perform his or her accompaniment and explain whether the purpose was to preserve or to change the original song.

Indicators of Success

- Students create arrangements that either preserve or reinterpret the song.

- Students accurately perform the new accompaniment and explain how it is appropriate.

(continued)

Follow-up

- Play recordings for students of two stylistically different arrangements of a song—for example, the Beatles' original recording of "With a Little Help from My Friends" and Joe Cocker's version of the song; or the Doors' original recording of "Light My Fire" and José Feliciano's version of the song. Ask them to explain how the arrangements are different.

STANDARD 4C

Composing and arranging music within specified guidelines: Students compose and arrange music for voices and various acoustic and electronic instruments, demonstrating knowledge of the ranges and traditional usages of the sound sources.

Objective

- Students will compose a song in a popular or folk style for acoustic guitar and voice or for two acoustic guitars.

Materials

- Recordings or sheet music for selected pop or folk songs
- Audio-playback equipment, if recordings are used
- Manuscript paper

Prior Knowledge and Experiences

- Students can play first-position major, major-seventh, minor, minor-seventh, and dominant-seventh chords and their barre-chord counterparts.
- Students can play several beginning- to intermediate-level accompaniment patterns.
- Students can compose and notate simple melodies using conventional music notation.
- Students can notate chord progressions using "slash" notation.
- Students have been introduced to chord functions in a major key and to the use of borrowed dominants and cadences.
- Students have been introduced to the formal elements of a pop or folk song (verse, chorus, bridge, coda).

Procedures

1. Review with students the formal elements of pop and folk songs and analyze two or three examples.

2. Have each student compose a song using a given form, all students using the same form; for example: introduction (eight measures), verse 1 (sixteen measures), chorus (eight measures), verse 2 (sixteen measures), chorus (eight measures), bridge (eight measures), chorus (eight measures), coda (four measures).

3. Help students identify an appropriate key, style, and tempo for their songs. Then assist them in determining the proper chords to be used based on the key of their choice. Limit the chords to I, ii, iii, IV, V, and vi in the chosen key and borrowed dominants V/V, V/ii, and V/IV. [*Note:* Chord extensions such as minor sevenths may be used if students can play them.] Give careful instruction in the proper use of cadences in the chosen key and in the selected borrowed dominant chords.

4. Have students begin drafts of their songs by writing a melody and adding chords, or vice versa. Once their drafts are completed, assist them in notating their songs properly. Explain that they should use a lead-sheet format with a two-staff system—the top staff for the melody and the bottom staff for the chord changes, using slash notation. If the melody is to be sung (rather than being performed by a second guitarist), tell them they may write lyrics at this time. Emphasize creativity within the given form, but encourage students to keep their songs simple.

5. Once you have made suggestions and corrections, have students complete final drafts and perform their songs for the class.

Indicators of Success

- Students compose in the given form and accurately notate their songs so that they can be performed by others.

Follow-up

- Play for students a recorded piece that uses the form studied, and ask them to write the name for each section as they hear it.

STANDARD 5B

Reading and notating music: Students sightread, accurately and expressively, music with a level of difficulty of 3, on a scale of 1 to 6.

Objective

- Students will develop first-position sightreading skills by playing ensemble pieces with a level of difficulty of 3.

Materials

- *Music for 3 and 4 Guitars,* volume 1, by Paul Gerrits (San Francisco: Doberman/Guitar Solo Publications, 1977)

Prior Knowledge and Experiences

- Students have played first-position melodies.
- Students can sightread music with a level of difficulty of 2.

Procedures

1. Divide the class into a three-section ensemble. To ensure good balance, place stronger players strategically throughout the ensemble.

2. Have students warm up by sightreading one or two simple trios (nos. 1, 2, 7, 10) from *Music for 3 or 4 Guitars.* Assign each section to one of the trio parts, and have students play through the piece twice; each time, reassign parts so that each section has the opportunity to sightread each part. [*Note:* This format can be followed with any sightreading materials, using any number of sections in the ensemble.]

3. Help students develop guidelines for sightreading, such as the following:

   - keep up with the tempo, even if it means "dropping" a note;
   - use a counting or time-keeping system;
   - visually scan the music to "hear" it in the "inner ear";
   - find opportunities to scan the music, such as when the teacher is working with other students;
   - silently "feel" the pitches with the fingers; and
   - visually scan dynamics and other markings, aiming for an expressive reading.

4. Have students sightread a tune of slightly higher degree of difficulty (nos. 5, 6). Then have students sightread ensembles 4 and 12, in that order.

5. Reorganize the class into four sections to sightread one of the quartet ensembles in this volume (nos. 3, 8, 9, 10). When the score displays two voices on one staff, as in number 8, ask one section to play the up-stem voice and another the down-stem voice. Have advanced players attempt reading both parts at once, if they wish. [*Note:* Song 9 can be played entirely in first position with the exception of the high A in part 1.]

Indicators of Success

- Students expressively sightread ensemble music, with a level of difficulty of 3, with reasonable accuracy and at appropriate tempos.

Follow-up

- Have students sightread one or two pieces as part of their warm-up activities for each class.

STANDARD 5D

Reading and notating music: Students interpret nonstandard notation symbols used by some 20th-century composers.

Objective

■ Students will interpret symbols used in notating twentieth-century music.

Materials

■ "Fantasia de los Econs," from *Acerca del Cielo: Guitar Ensemble,* by Leo Brouwer, eight- or twenty-four-part (Doberman, Inc., CP 2021, St-Nicholas Est, Quebec, Canada G7A 4X5; telephone 418-831-1304)

■ Chalkboard or transparency with nonstandard notation symbols (see step 2)

■ Overhead projector, if transparency is used

Prior Knowledge and Experiences

■ Students can perform several right-hand techniques with facility.

Procedures

1. Assist students as they scan through the music for "Fantasia de los Econs." Have them look for symbols that are unusual or that they cannot interpret, such as, "pst, sssh" [sounds made with mouth]; ↑ [as high as possible]; M.G. [*MIT GLAS:* Hold a glass on the strings at the indicated position].

2. Using the chalkboard or a transparency with the nonstandard notation symbols from the piece, discuss the proper interpretation of each symbol. Entertain all ideas as to the correct performance technique for each symbol.

3. After the correct interpretation is reached, model the execution of the passages or notes that use difficult techniques. Then have students practice these examples.

4. Rehearse the entire composition, focusing on cohesive performance of the new techniques.

5. Discuss with students the aural and artistic effects of the various techniques in the piece.

Indicators of Success

■ Students identify and interpret nonstandard notation symbols.

■ Students perform "Fantasia de los Econs" with reasonable technical proficiency and understanding.

Follow-up

■ Play for students the recording of "Fantasia de los Econs," from *Acerca del Cielo: Guitar Ensemble* (University of Quebec Guitar Ensemble, Leo Brouwer, Doberman DO 179), asking students to compare their interpretation of the nontraditional notation symbols with the composer's interpretation that they hear on the recording.

■ Have students develop a notational symbol for a nontraditional technique that they create on their guitar (playing behind the nut, dragging the pick up or down the strings, playing the guitar with a violin bow, and so on). Have this symbol include, as applicable, duration and pitch.

STANDARD 6A

Listening to, analyzing, and describing music: Students analyze aural examples of a varied repertoire of music, representing diverse genres and cultures, by describing the uses of elements of music and expressive devices.

Objective

- Students will identify and describe the elements of music and techniques they hear in performances in different styles.

Materials

- Teacher-generated worksheet allowing space for students to write information about guitar techniques and the uses of elements of music (see steps 1 and 2)

- Recorded examples of two or three guitar styles unfamiliar to students, from, for example, *The Guitar Player Presents: Legends of Guitar* (Rhino R270563), which includes two volumes for most styles: classical (one volume), jazz, electric blues, country, surf (one volume), 50s rock, 60s rock, 70s rock

- Audio-playback equipment

Prior Knowledge and Experiences

- Students have listened to many guitar recordings in different styles.

Procedures

1. Play a recording of one of the selected examples, asking students to listen for techniques used on the recording. Then distribute the worksheet, and using the listening as a point of reference, review the elements of music and the guitar techniques listed on the worksheet.

2. Have students listen to the recording again. Ask them to write terms (not sentences) that identify the unique features of the music; that is, uses of elements of music and guitar techniques. Discuss and replay as necessary. [*Note:* Students may also list the title and the guitarist as an aid to remembering the composition, but encourage them to focus mainly on elements of music and guitar techniques.]

3. Play one or two additional selections and have students listen to them and analyze them as in step 2.

4. Have students, using their individual handouts, summarize the similarities and differences between the styles they have heard.

Indicators of Success

- Students accurately analyze and describe the musical elements and techniques in guitar performances.

Follow-up

- Have students identify the use of different techniques and of elements of music in the career development of a particular guitarist.

- Have students listen to performances on guitar (and on related string instruments) from different classical periods and styles. Ask them to analyze and identify what they hear.

STANDARD 6A

Listening to, analyzing, and describing music: Students analyze aural examples of a varied repertoire of music, representing diverse genres and cultures, by describing the uses of elements of music and expressive devices.

Objective

- Students will aurally identify techniques for altering pitch and sustaining sound on the Chinese pipa and recreate them in a guitar ensemble piece.

Materials

- Recording of "Fe Hua Dian Cui," by Lui Pui-Yuen, on *Music of the Chinese Pi'Pa,* Nonesuch 702085-2; or "Hero's Defeat," on *Music Resources for Multicultural Perspectives,* 2d ed., Music Educators National Conference CD #3017

- "Folk Melody," arr. Romana Hartmetz, two-part, in *Guitar Ensembles,* intermediate level, by Nancy Marsters, Leo Welch, and Romana Hartmetz (Tallahassee, FL: Class Guitar Resources, 1996)

- Photograph of pipa and player, in *Multicultural Perspectives in Music Education,* 2d ed., edited by William M. Anderson and Patricia Shehan Campbell (Reston, VA: Music Educators National Conference, 1996)

- Map including both China and Vietnam

- Audio-playback equipment

Procedures

1. Have the class discuss and play some special effects guitar players use, including a "bend" in blues or rock and the pick-style tremolo used in bluegrass mandolin technique.

2. Display the photograph of the pipa and a pipa player. Explain that bends and tremolos are common techniques on this instrument from China. Have students note the number of strings and frets, as well as the nearly vertical position of the instrument. Point out that the pipa is a lute with a round back.

3. Play the recording of "Fe Hua Dian Cui" or "Hero's Defeat," and have students indicate when they hear a tremolo. Mention that because the pipa sound dies away quickly, the tremolo technique, in which the strings are plucked repetitively, helps provide a nearly continuous sound.

4. Replay the recording, having students listen for the quarter-tone pitch bends, noticing when they occur in a phrase [on long notes]. Also, have students speculate on how a bend is achieved on the pipa. [The finger depresses the string past the visual contact point.]

5. Have students try each technique on the guitar, imitating the sound of the pipa. Discuss with them how these techniques are the same as (or different from) the techniques explored in step 1.

6. Refer students to "Folk Melody" and mention that the techniques they have been discussing are also used in some Vietnamese music, such as this piece. Display a map of China and Vietnam, and have students notice their proximity. Explain that at one time, China annexed Vietnam, and, therefore, some aspects of the two countries' cultures are similar.

7. Have students play through "Folk Melody" and then apply the pitch bends and tremolo at appropriate places. Discuss with students how well they are imitating the sound of the pipa. Continue rehearsing as appropriate.

Indicators of Success

- Students aurally identify pitch bend and tremolo techniques on the pipa and successfully reproduce them on guitar.

Prior Knowledge and Experiences

- Students have facility playing free strokes (not allowing the right-hand finger to come to rest against a lower adjacent string).

- Students can read and play music up to the fifth position.

- Students have sightread "Folk Melody."

- Students describe the pipa and contrast it with the guitar.

Follow-up

- Have students identify and play the pitch bends or tremolo in different styles of music, such as bluegrass mandolin, Russian balalaika, and American blues or rock. Then give them the opportunity to apply these techniques in a simple melody from the culture.

STANDARD 6C

Listening to, analyzing, and describing music: Students identify and explain compositional devices and techniques used to provide unity and variety and tension and release in a musical work and give examples of other works that make similar uses of these devices and techniques.

Objective

- Students will identify uses of unity and variety and tension and release in a guitar ensemble selection.

Materials

- "Brazilian Bossa," three-part (lead, chords, bass) in *H.O.T. Hands-On Training: Second-Year Guitar* by Leo Welch and Nancy Marsters (Tallahassee, FL: Class Guitar Resources, 1992)

Prior Knowledge and Experiences

- Students can play sixteenth-note rhythms accurately.
- Students can read simple melodic lines in upper positions.
- Students can play jazz chord forms.

Procedures

1. Help students learn the A section of "Brazilian Bossa." As they rehearse it, isolate and have them practice the repeated rhythmic and melodic motifs. Lead them to discover that these repeating ideas tie the composition together. Also, note that the repeated rhythms in the bass line serve the same purpose.

2. Work with the solo B section next. Help students discover how this section is different, melodically and rhythmically, from the highly organized rhythms and motifs of the A section. At the end of the B section, identify the modulation and help students determine its purpose [to build tension before the familiar A section returns].

3. Form rehearsal groups and have students prepare the music so that the unifying elements and the modulation are evident in their performance.

4. Have groups perform for the class, asking the class to evaluate each group's performance.

Indicators of Success

- Students identify uses of unity and variety and tension and release in the sections of "Brazilian Bossa" and apply this knowledge to a musical performance.

Follow-up

- Have students explore unity and variety in the following ensembles from *H.O.T. Hands-On Training: Second-Year Guitar:* "Guy's Minuet," "Big Piece," "Gavottes I and II," and "Minuet and Trio" (all in ternary form).

STANDARD 6E

Listening to, analyzing, and describing music: Students compare ways in which musical materials are used in a given example relative to ways in which they are used in other works of the same genre or style.

Objective

- Students will compare rock-guitar voicings in two songs and describe the effects on the character and flow of the music.

Materials

- Student-generated lead sheets for "Basket Case" by Green Day and "Afternoons and Coffeespoons" by Crash Test Dummies

- Audiocassette recorder, microphone, and blank cassette

Prior Knowledge and Experiences

- Students can read and perform many first-position chords, "power chords" (see step 2), and some barre chords.

- Students have listened to recordings of "Basket Case," on *Dookie,* Reprise Records 945529-2, and "Afternoons and Coffeespoons," on *God Shuffled His Feet,* Arista Records 74321-16531-2.

- Students have created lead sheets (simply lyrics and chords, for example) for "Basket Case" and "Afternoons and Coffeespoons."

Procedures

1. Have students review "Basket Case" and "Afternoons and Coffeespoons," using the lead sheets they have made. Then record their playing.

2. Introduce students to power chord fingerings for C, F, and G, explaining that the power chord (a movable form) is a modified barre chord that uses two or three strings (root + fifth; or root + fifth + octave). Then explain that there are two basic forms of power chords—one with the root of the chord on the sixth string, the other with the root on the fifth string.

Movable Two-Note Power Chords		Movable Three-Note Power Chords	
Root on Sixth	Root on Fifth	Root on Sixth	Root on Fifth

x = do not play
circled nos. = fingerings

root on string 6, fret 1 = F
root on string 6, fret 3 = G
root on string 5, fret 3 = C

3. Have students practice both fingerings for the two-note chords and the three-note chords. Then have them decide whether to use the two-note or three-note versions and whether to use the form with the root on the sixth string or the fifth string. Ask them to practice the selected chords using a pick to strum a single down-stroke for each chord, strumming only the strings that are fingered.

4. When students are secure in playing the power chords, have them perform "Basket Case" as a group. Record the ensemble again. Play the recording and have students compare this performance with the one from step 1. Ask them why and how changing the voicings of the guitar chords changed the character of the song so much. Also, ask how that change affected the character and flow of the music.

(continued)

5. Have students review the power chords for "Afternoons and Coffeespoons" (same chords as "Basket Case") and record their playing.

6. Play the recordings of both of their performances of "Afternoons and Coffeespoons." Have students decide why and how they are contrasting (see step 4).

7. Have students listen to both of their performances of the two songs and briefly summarize their former analyses.

Indicators of Success

■ Students play different chord voicings in two songs and compare and contrast the results.

Follow-up

■ Have students learn power chords in a key other than C and perform and compare two songs in that key, as in the procedures above.

STANDARD 7A

Evaluating music and music performances: Students evolve specific criteria for making informed, critical evaluations of the quality and effectiveness of performances, compositions, arrangements, and improvisations and apply the criteria in their personal participation in music.

Objective

- Students develop performance criteria and use these criteria to evaluate and improve their performances.

Materials

- Solo and duet pieces from student text or other guitar publications
- Videocamera and blank videotape
- Videocassette player and monitor
- Chalkboard

Prior Knowledge and Experiences

- Students have been practicing solos or duets, but they have not yet polished their performances.

Procedures

1. Explain to students that in this class session they will develop specific criteria that will help them polish their performances of the pieces they have been practicing. Begin a discussion to help them differentiate between musical, technical, and nonmusical aspects.

2. As the discussion proceeds, list criteria, such as the following, on the chalkboard:

Expression

- accurate tempo
- appropriate dynamics
- correct phrasing
- consistency of all of the above
- balance of parts in a duet

Technical

- accurate pitch
- accurate rhythm
- "clean" and coordinated finger work
- correct hand and body position
- consistency of all of the above

Nonmusical

- stage presence

3. Have students rehearse their solos or duets, taking into account the criteria developed in steps 1 and 2. Circulate among students to assist and advise.

4. Reassemble the group and, using a previously organized mock "concert hall" setting in the classroom, have several students perform solos or duets as you videotape the performances.

5. Have students view the videotape and critique the performances according to the criteria they have developed. Ask each student (or duo) to jot down some things he or she did well and some ways the performance could be improved.

(continued)

Indicators of Success

- Students develop appropriate evaluation criteria.
- Students analyze their videotaped performances, using the criteria they have developed.
- Students identify how they can improve their performances for a forthcoming concert.

Follow-up

- Have students view a videotape of their formal concert and analyze to what degree they have met their established criteria.
- Guide students in editing their evaluative criteria for future use.

STANDARD 7A

Evaluating music and music performances: Students evolve specific criteria for making informed, critical evaluations of the quality and effectiveness of performances, compositions, arrangements, and improvisations and apply the criteria in their personal participation in music.

Objective

- Students develop criteria for evaluating individual and group ensemble skills and apply them to their performance in a duet, trio, or quartet.

Materials

- Ensemble music (duet, trio, or quartet) from any guitar method book

Prior Knowledge and Experiences

- Students can read and play pitches on all six strings up to the fifth fret.
- Students have been assigned to groups of like (or mixed) ability, and they have learned their ensemble parts for the selected piece.

Procedures

1. Organize students into duos, trios, or quartets in which they have been rehearsing the selected piece.

2. Have each group select a leader and agree on the leader's responsibilities, such as starting and stopping, initiating and mediating decisions about music expression and technique, and keeping a consistent tempo.

3. Explain to students that their assignment is to play their parts in the ensemble piece and to discuss and agree upon criteria for rating their performance. Help students, as a class, develop (and remember) some criteria such as:

    - performing parts, individually, with accuracy of pitch, rhythm, and tempo;
    - demonstrating, individually, an efficient use of practice time;
    - maintaining cohesive intonation and rhythm and a consistent tempo as an ensemble;
    - listening to one another and communicating the agreed-upon expression (such as tempo and dynamics); or
    - being silent just before and after their performance, and beginning and ending together.

4. Have students tune their instruments. Establish a time limit for the group rehearsal. Move between groups to assist as appropriate, including reviewing pitch and rhythm in each group's ensemble as necessary.

5. Ask each ensemble to perform for the class, with the other groups assessing the performance according to the established criteria.

Indicators of Success

- Students develop and apply criteria for evaluating ensemble practice and performance.
- Students use the criteria they have developed to accurately evaluate their own and others' performances.

(continued)

Follow-up

- Videotape the students' performance (see step 5) for further review and evaluation.
- Have students attend a professional ensemble rehearsal or performance, or watch an appropriate videotape, and compare what they hear to their class effort in the procedures above.

STANDARD 8A

Understanding relationships between music, the other arts, and disciplines outside the arts:
*Students explain how elements, artistic processes, and organizational principles are used
in similar and distinctive ways in the various arts and cite examples.*

Objective

- Students will identify and describe how elements and organizational principles are used in two art forms.

Materials

- "Fiesta en Jerez," an Andalusian flamenco, performed by guitarist Pepe Romero, on *Flamenco!*, Mercury Living Prescence CD-434 361-2

- Print reproduction or slide of painting "View of Toledo" by El Greco

- Audio-playback equipment

- Slide projector, if slide is used

- Map showing Spain and the Mediterranean Sea (including Crete, the Middle East, and North Africa)

- Chalkboard

Prior Knowledge and Experiences

- Students can identify and describe the elements of music (pitch, rhythm, harmony, dynamics, timbre, texture, and form).

- Students can identify and describe the organizational principles of music (such as unity and variety or repetition and contrast).

Procedures

1. Play an excerpt from the recording of "Fiesta en Jerez," and have students identify it as flamenco music. Lead students in a brief discussion of flamenco guitar techniques that are familiar to them, such as *rasgueado.* Have a student locate Spain and the city of Jerez (pronounced "heh-RETH") on the map and then identify the southerly area called Andalusia (from the Muslim "al Andalus," meaning all the land controlled by Islam).

2. Display "View of Toledo" (the Spanish city where the painter El Greco lived). Tell students that El Greco was born Domenico Theotocopuli (1541–1614) on Crete, and he spent his life in Spain. Ask a student to locate Toledo, near Madrid, on the map. Briefly discuss with students what they know about the arts and history of Spain.

3. Review the organizational principles of music. Then, leaving the painting in view, replay "Fiesta en Jerez," asking students to identify the music's organizational principles. After the listening, in a vertical column on the chalkboard, write key terms students mention, such as strongly contrasting dynamics, tessitura, and timbre; improvisation. Expand the discussion to note how the elements of music are used—for example, fast, metrical tempo.

4. Referring to "View of Toledo," review and discuss the elements of visual arts. Have students suggest how some of these elements are related to elements of music. Review the organizational principles of visual arts.

5. Ask students to study the painting and identify how the elements of the visual arts are used—for example, contrast (strongly contrasting color, light, and form; no shape repeated exactly). Write the key words they mention on the chalkboard. Ask them what mood results from the way the elements are used (somber; intense; agitated). Have them discuss whether, and how, the prevailing mood of the music and the painting are similar.

6. Have students summarize their analyses, referring to the lists on the chalkboard. Ask them to speculate on why the music and art are similar. Mention that the painting is from the intensely religious period of the Inquisition, and that flamenco originated from a persecuted gypsy minority.

(continued)

- Students can identify and describe the elements of the visual arts (such as line, texture, color, form, value, and space).

- Students can identify and describe the organizational principles of the visual arts (such as repetition, balance, emphasis, contrast, and unity).

Indicators of Success

- Students identify and compare how elements and organizational principles of art and music are used in flamenco guitar music and a painting by El Greco.

Follow-up

- From the *Flamenco!* recording, have students listen to Romero's rendition of "Recuerdos de la Alhambra" by Francisco Tárrega or to Spanish Dance no. 5, "Andaluza," by Enrico Granados. Then have them view slides of the Alhambra in Granada, similarly comparing organizational principles and elements used in the music and the architecture.

- Lead students in a discussion exploring judgments (such as good versus bad, and pleasant versus unpleasant) that they may have made while describing and comparing the elements of the two arts in the procedures above. Introduce and define the term "aesthetics," and have students discuss how judgments can be influenced by subjectivity, education, and so forth.

STANDARD 8C

Understanding relationships between music, the other arts, and disciplines outside the arts:
Students explain ways in which the principles and subject matter of various disciplines
outside the arts are interrelated with those of music.

Objective

- Students will identify strophic form in both music and poetry, performing songs and studying poems in that form.

Materials

- Selected songs in strophic form, including "Amazing Grace" and "If I Had a Hammer" or "Green, Green Grass of Home," all in *Get America Singing . . . Again!,* compiled by Music Educators National Conference (Milwaukee: Hal Leonard Corporation, 1996)
- Recordings of Schubert lieder, such as "To Music" or "The Trout," performed by Bryn Terfel, on *An die Musik,* Deutsche Grammophon CD-445 294-2
- Audio-playback equipment
- Poetry organized in strophic form (for example, "The Chimney Sweeper" or "The Tyger" by William Blake; "I Felt a Funeral in My Brain" by Emily Dickinson)
- Chalkboard

Prior Knowledge and Experiences

- Students have played a chordal accompaniment to "Amazing Grace."

Procedures

1. Review the song "Amazing Grace" with students, having students concentrate on the text. Write the words on the chalkboard, review the rhyme scheme, and define "strophe."

2. Explain how strophic form is a simple form used both by poets and musicians. Play an example of Schubert lieder and invite discussion on the many types of popular music that use this form.

3. Have students examine the song "If I Had a Hammer" or "Green, Green Grass of Home," identify the form as strophic, and explain the reasons for their decision. In a similar fashion, have students identify a poem as being in strophic form.

4. Guide students in a discussion of how the music and poetry of a given song are complementary or contrasting (meter, syllabic rhythm, expression, and so on).

Indicators of Success

- Students identify strophic form in poetry and music examples and justify their decisions.

Follow-up

- Ask students to create their own strophic poem (from poetry in the public domain) and set it to music. Then have them notate and record their song.

- Play a recording of a work in through-composed form (for example, Franz Schubert's narrative ballad "The Erlking"), and have students describe how the form differs from that of the strophic Schubert lieder they have heard.

STANDARD 9A

Understanding music in relation to history and culture: Students classify by genre or style and by historical period or culture unfamiliar but representative aural examples of music and explain the reasoning behind their classifications.

Objective

- Students will identify musical and technical elements, style, and place of origin for Mexican and Mexican American music.

Materials

- Recordings of three unfamiliar pieces in different styles: a song featuring mariachi, such as those on *Mas Canciones,* performed by Linda Ronstadt, Elektra 61239-2; a song featuring guitars from a Los Lobos album; or an example of *conjuncto,* Mexican *corrido,* or a ballad accompanied by guitar, such as "El Caballa Blanco" or "De colores"
- Audio-playback equipment
- Chalkboard

Prior Knowledge and Experiences

- Students have experience analyzing and identifying pieces in different Mexican guitar styles, such as mariachi, corrido, and *jarana,* and contemporary Mexican American styles, such as conjuncto and commercial pop.
- Students have collected information about Mexican and Mexican American guitar styles in their notebooks.

Procedures

1. Have the class review, using their notebooks, Mexican and Mexican American guitar styles and the elements and playing techniques associated with each. Write key words on the chalkboard. Include the following points in the review:

   - type of guitar, European or Mexican (European—nylon-string classical, steel-string acoustic, solid-body electric; Mexican—vihuela, guitarrón, charanga);

   - playing techniques used, such as pick, fingerstyle, strumming, or *rasgueado;*

   - accompanying instruments, such as violin or harp;

   - form of piece;

   - type of harmony, such as parallel thirds, complexity of chord progression;

   - name of the style; and

   - country of origin.

2. Explain to students that they are going to hear three unfamiliar pieces, and that they should use the items listed in step 1 to analyze and identify each style. Have them use a separate sheet of paper for each selection. Play the recordings, allowing students enough time to write their notes for each.

3. On a separate sheet of paper, have students write their name and the numbers 1, 2, and 3, along with the style name and country of origin for each selection. After they have identified the selections, collect the sheets and quickly review them for accuracy.

4. Lead the class in a discussion of the three pieces, having students use their notes from the listening. Replay the pieces during the discussion, as needed, to make specific points.

Indicators of Success

- Students identify musical and technical elements, style, and place of origin for selected Mexican and Mexican American music.
- Students explain the reasoning for their classifications.

Follow-up

- Have students identify the style of music for other guitar-like instruments they have studied, such as pipa, lute, and sitar.

- Have students analyze music by invited guitar players who play music in a variety of styles.

STANDARD 9B

Understanding music in relation to history and culture: Students identify sources of American music genres, trace the evolution of those genres, and cite well-known musicians associated with them.

Objective

- Students will identify African American and European American characteristics in American folk and rock music and place the music in its historical context.

Materials

- *A Tribute to Woody Guthrie & Leadbelly,* student text and teacher's guide, by Will Schmid (Reston, VA: Music Educators National Conference [MENC], 1991)

- Video recording *Folkways: A Vision Shared,* CBS Music Video Enterprises, 1988 (available from MENC)

- Audio recording *Folkways: The Original Vision,* Smithsonian/Folkways, SF 40001 (available from MENC)

- Chalkboard

Prior Knowledge and Experiences

- Students can play a 12-bar blues chord progression in D major.

Procedures

1. From lead sheets in the student text, have students sing and play the following songs for a brief review: "I Ain't Got No Home" and "The Midnight Special" or "Rock Island Line." Lead students in a discussion of the words to each song, asking them to decide how the words are closely related to the time and place of their origin. Help them decide how the words depict the experiences of different groups in America.

2. Have students listen to the Guthrie and Leadbelly performances of these songs on the recording *The Original Vision.* Then have students compare them to performances of the same songs by Bruce Springsteen ("I Ain't Got No Home") and Taj Mahal ("The Midnight Special") or Little Richard ("Rock Island Line") on the video *Folkways: A Vision Shared.* Use the style chart in the student text (page 8) to lead students in a discussion of characteristics of some of the following: tone quality, melody, rhythm, tempo, and words. Help students associate the various style characteristics with either African American or European American musical style. Ask students to list them on the chalkboard and in their notebooks.

3. Briefly outline for students the contents of chapter 1, "African and European Roots of American Music," in the student text.

4. Introduce the songs "Deportee" and "The Bourgeois Blues" in the student text, having students read and discuss the lyrics. Then have students practice the chords, rhythms, and melodies until they can perform the songs satisfactorily.

5. Show students the portions of the video in which Emmylou Harris and Arlo Guthrie perform "Deportee" and Taj Mahal performs "The Bourgeois Blues." Help students identify and write down the African American and European American characteristics of these songs (as in step 2). Include a discussion of the raspy vocal quality derived from Africa that is favored by many rock vocalists.

Indicators of Success

- Students identify African American and European American characteristics in American folk and rock music, placing selected Guthrie and Leadbelly songs in their historical context.

- Students can sing and play "I Ain't Got No Home" by Woody Guthrie and "The Midnight Special" or "Rock Island Line" by Leadbelly, from lead sheets in *A Tribute to Woody Guthrie & Leadbelly*, student text.

- Students have viewed the introductory material on the video *Folkways: A Vision Shared*.

Follow-up

- Have students identify and experiment with the "bass-after" and "boom-chick" guitar strums in Guthrie's "Union Maid" from lead sheets in *A Tribute to Woody Guthrie and Leadbelly*, student text. Discuss with them how these strums later became part of bluegrass and country styles played by Doc Watson and Willie Nelson. Show them Pete Seeger's performance of "Union Maid" on the video *Folkways: A Vision Shared*, and assign reading in chapter 3, "Leadbelly," of the student text so they can learn more about these styles, techniques, and performers and their place in American history.

- Have students review the origin of the blues and then create their own blues lyrics, using as a model "Lonesome Rider Blues" (see Teacher's Guide Master #11, in *A Tribute to Woody Guthrie & Leadbelly*, teacher's guide).

STANDARD 9C

Understanding music in relation to history and culture: Students identify various roles
that musicians perform, cite representative individuals who have functioned in each role,
and describe their activities and achievements.

Objective

- Students will identify lawful uses of copyrighted materials and explain the interrelated roles of composer, lyricist, publisher, performer, agent, and record company.

Materials

- Copyright information resources, such as *Copyright: The Complete Guide for Music Educators,* 2d ed., by Jay Althouse (Van Nuys, CA: Alfred Publishing Company, 1997), available from MENC; "Copyright Law and Sound Recordings" by Robert H. Woody III, *Music Educators Journal* 80, no. 6 (May 1994); "In Retrospect—Copyright and Campfires" by Charles Gary, *Teaching Music* 4, no. 3 (December 1996)
- Chalkboard

Prior Knowledge and Experiences

- Students have been introduced to the function of copyright and the format of a copyright notice.

Procedures

1. Briefly review the function of copyright, citing examples of lawful (and unlawful) use of copyrighted materials (see Materials).

2. Ask some of the students to tell the class about the pieces they have selected (see Prior Knowledge and Experiences), having them identify the year of publication, whether the piece is an arrangement, and so on. Tell the class that in this lesson they are going to discuss the legal status of their pieces, considering the following categories:

   - public domain;
   - protected by a current copyright;
   - once protected by a copyright, which has expired; or
   - creation that is not yet protected.

3. Lead students in a discussion of the factors that will help them identify which category is appropriate for their selected pieces. Then, having students work in small groups, ask them to discuss with their group members what they think the status of their pieces is and why.

4. Have class reassemble. Discuss with them what use they could make of a piece of music that is protected, considering the following possibilities:

   - play it for themselves;
   - play it in a school concert for parents;
   - play it in a local restaurant;
   - play it for scouts at a Boy Scouts of America camp; or
   - make a recording for distribution.

5. Guide students in listing on the chalkboard various roles in the music business, such as composer, lyricist, performer, publisher, and music agent. Have them identify ways in which these roles are interdependent and how copyright protection is important to all of these people.

6. Have students consider when music that was copyrighted before 1922 went into the public domain.

7. Briefly summarize the importance of the various aspects of copyright the class has discussed.

- Students have studied how, why, and by whom a copyright is filed and have been introduced to a sample US copyright form. [*Note:* Form PA, with instructions, is available from the Forms Hotline (telephone 202-707-9100).]

- Students have each selected a piece they would like to learn to play on the guitar (see step 2).

Indicators of Success

- Students interpret the meaning of a copyright notice on the music they play.

- Students describe aspects of the interrelated roles of composer, lyricist, publisher, performer, agent, and record companies.

Follow-up

- Have students determine whether the copyrights for the songs in *Get America Singing . . . Again!,* compiled by Music Educators National Conference (Milwaukee: Hal Leonard Corporation, 1996), are of the original music, the words, or the arrangement.

STANDARD 9D

Understanding music in relation to history and culture: Students identify and explain the stylistic features of a given musical work that serve to define its aesthetic tradition and its historical or cultural context.

Objective

- Students will identify elements in reggae style and in the forms that preceded and influenced reggae (mento, rhythm and blues, ska, and rock steady), perform the "back-beat" rhythm, and describe the Jamaican historical and culture context of reggae.

Materials

- Recording of "Hallelujah Time" or "I Shot the Sheriff," performed by Bob Marley and the Wailers, on *Burnin',* Tuff Gong/Island 422-846200

- Recordings *Roots of Reggae: Ska,* Rhino CD 72438; and *Roots of Reggae: Rock Steady,* Rhino CD 72439

- Recording of "Mango Time" (mento), on *Caribbean Island Music,* Elektra/Nonesuch 72047

- Selected rhythm and blues recordings of Otis Redding, Sam Cooke, or Brook Benton

- Audio-playback equipment

- Map of the Caribbean and the southeastern United States

- Chalkboard

Procedures

1. Play a reggae recording (see Materials) and help students identify reggae by its distinctive rhythms: the prominent bass "riddim," the "back-beat" emphasis on beats 2 and 4, and the "laid-back" (moderate) tempo. Also review the form, harmony, lyrics, and vocal style of reggae.

2. Teach students how to play the back-beat rhythm. On a single chord, have students play down and up strums in 4/4 meter, first using quarter notes and then eighth notes. Then have students insert a rest on beats 1 and 3, playing down and up eighth notes on beats 2 and 4. To create the silence required by the rest, have students dampen the strings, rotating the right hand clockwise (toward the bridge) so that the little finger and side of the hand touch all strings, thus stopping vibration and sound.

3. Display a map of the Caribbean, having students identify Jamaica and its neighbors and note Jamaica's proximity to Florida. Present key information about Jamaica's history. Explain that Jamaica was colonized by the Spanish in the sixteenth century, and the first African slaves were brought to the island at that time. Note that in a conflict from 1655 to 1660, the British conquered Jamaica. During the war, many slaves took to the mountains and began a long fight for independence, and they came to be known as the Maroons. Have students decide how reggae's lyrics reflect the social conditions of Jamaica.

4. On the chalkboard, draw a diagram showing the styles and elements that influenced reggae. Play an excerpt of each style:

   mento (rhumba rhythm) + R & B ("slick" vocal harmonies)
   ↓
   ska (early 60s: vibrant, dance music)
   ↓
   rock steady (about 1966–68: steadier beat and slower tempo than ska; lyrics reflecting social consciousness)
   ↓
   reggae (about 1968: slower tempo than rock steady; lyrics more serious than in ska, reflecting modern Jamaican religious thinking)

5. Summarize with students what they have learned about reggae, its historical and cultural roots, and its musical predecessors. Review the back-beat rhythm.

Prior Knowledge and Experiences

- Students have experience playing blues.
- Students have studied the influence of African music on the music of the western hemisphere.

Indicators of Success

- Students identify the elements of reggae style.
- Students identify and describe how other forms (mento, rhythm and blues, ska, rock steady) influenced reggae.
- Students accurately perform the back-beat rhythm.
- Students describe Jamaican history and culture in relation to reggae and its creators.

Follow-up

- Have students compose a reggae over a given chord progression, incorporating suitable strums and creating lyrics in the reggae style.

STANDARD 9E

Understanding music in relation to history and culture: Students identify and describe music genres or styles that show the influence of two or more cultural traditions, identify the cultural source of each influence, and trace the historical conditions that produced the synthesis of influences.

Objective

- Students will identify African and European elements of blues in a blues vocal and in a jazz composition, name some key blues performers, and play the blues shuffle strum.

Materials

- Recording of "Poor Man's Blues," composed and performed by Bessie Smith (1894?–1937), on *Bessie Smith: The Complete Recordings,* vol. 4, Columbia C2K 52838
- Recording of "Main Stem" by Edward "Duke" Ellington (1899–1974), on *Duke Ellington: The Blanton-Webster Band,* RCA CD-5659-2-RB
- Chalkboard
- Audio-playback equipment

Prior Knowledge and Experiences

- Students can play the E-major blues progression.
- Students have listened to several styles of African music, and they can identify elements and organizational principles in the music.

Procedures

1. Lead students in reviewing the 12-bar blues pattern in E major, having them play four down strums per measure.

2. Using only the E chord, demonstrate the straight-eighth strum commonly used in rock styles; strum down on each number and up on each "+": 1+ 2+ 3+ 4+. Ask students to play along. When this becomes easy for them, demonstrate a blues shuffle rhythm by simply "swinging" both the count and the strum to create a triplet ♩♪ feeling; strum down on the quarter notes, up on the eighth notes. Have students repeat and practice until they can play it proficiently. [*Note:* Some students will improve their strumming if they dance to the shuffle rhythm.]

3. Ask students to name blues singers or guitarists they know or have studied, such as Leadbelly, B.B. King, Muddy Waters, or "Big" Bill Broonzy. Review what they know about blues (solo "sorrow songs"), its origin around the turn of the century, African influences on its style, and its profound influence on subsequent popular music.

4. Introduce the music of Bessie Smith, having students listen to "Poor Man's Blues." Review the African style elements they hear, noting each on the chalkboard. Replay the music periodically to revitalize the discussion, which should include the following elements: open, natural vocal style; portamento; flatted scale degrees; displaced accents; metronomic, slow tempo; call-and-response "dialogue" between singer and instrument(s); instrumental improvisation on the "response." Help students identify the main European-derived features (form, chord progression, instrumentation).

5. Introduce the music of Duke Ellington, having students listen to "Main Stem" (fast tempo, 12-bar form). Have students note the blues features and listen as the instruments "trade eights" (each playing eight measures in turn). Lead students in analyzing the elements, as they did in step 4.

6. Briefly have students summarize the history and elements of blues style mentioned above. Review the blues shuffle strum.

Indicators of Success

- Students accurately play the triplet unit of the blues shuffle strum.
- Students identify African and European elements of blues in a blues vocal and a jazz composition.
- Students name some key blues performers.

Follow-up

- Have students explore how the blues music they have studied in the procedures above relates to the historical conditions from which the music developed.
- Have students identify blues influences in rock and roll—for example, "That's All Right, Mama," by Arthur Crudup, performed by Elvis Presley; or "Crossroads," composed and recorded by Robert Johnson and the rock power trio Cream (featuring Eric Clapton).

RESOURCES

Music Referenced in This Text

"The Black Snake Wind" (Pima Indian text), arr. Mary Goetze. New York: Boosey & Hawkes. SSA. Level 2.

"Bourrée for Bach," from English Suite no. 2, transcribed by Bennett Williams. Santa Barbara, CA: Sam Fox. SA or TB.

"Echo Song" by Orlando di Lasso. Double chorus of mixed voices. Level 4. In *Five Centuries of Choral Music for Mixed Voices,* Book 1 (Milwaukee: Hal Leonard Corporation, 1941).

"Fantasia de los Econs," from *Acerca del Cielo: Guitar Ensemble,* by Leo Brouwer. Eight- or twenty-four-part. Doberman, Inc., CP 2021, St-Nicholas Est, Quebec, Canada G7A 4X5; telephone 418-831-1304.

"Mister Sandman" by Pat Ballard, arr. Ed Lojeski. Milwaukee: Hal Leonard Corporation. SATB. Level 4.

"What If I Never Speed," by John Dowland, transcribed by Peter Warlock. SATB. Level 4. In *Five Centuries of Choral Music for Mixed Voices,* Book 1 (Milwaukee: Hal Leonard Corporation, 1941).

Methods and Other Books Referenced in This Text

*Althouse, Jay. *Copyright: The Complete Guide for Music Educators,* 2d ed. Van Nuys, CA: Alfred Publishing Company, 1997.

*Anderson, William M., and Patricia S. Campbell, eds. *Multicultural Perspectives in Music Education,* 2d ed. Reston, VA: Music Educators National Conference, 1996.

Bay, Mel. *Mel Bay's Guitar Class Method,* vol. 1. Pacific, MO: Mel Bay, 1980. Book and recording.

Duncan, Charles. *Modern Approach to Classical Guitar,* Book 1. Milwaukee: Hal Leonard Corporation, 1996.

Ellis, Cathy. *Complete Guide for the Guitar.* Miami: Ellis Family Music, 1990.

Feldstein, Sandy, and Aaron Stang. *Guitar Ensemble,* Book 1. Belwin's 21st-Century Guitar Library. Miami: CPP Belwin/Warner Bros. Publications, 1994.

Gerrits, Paul. *Music for 3 and 4 Guitars,* vol. 1. San Francisco: Doberman/Guitar Solo Publications, 1977.

Hackett, Patricia. *The Melody Book: 300 Selections from the World of Music for Piano, Guitar, Autoharp, Recorder and Voice,* 3d ed. Upper Saddle River, NJ: Prentice-Hall, 1998.

Marsters, Nancy. *Explore It! Guitar and Style.* Tallahassee, FL: Class Guitar Resources, 1992.

Marsters, Nancy, Leo Welch, and Romana Hartmetz. *Guitar Ensembles,* intermediate level. Tallahassee, FL: Class Guitar Resources, 1996.

Music Educators National Conference, comp. *Get America Singing . . . Again!* Milwaukee: Hal Leonard Corporation, 1996.

Music and You, Grades K–8. New York: Macmillan/McGraw-Hill, 1991.

The Music Connection, Grades K–8. Parsippany, NJ: Silver Burdett Ginn, 1997.

Purse, Bill. *Mel Bay Presents Bach Chorales for Guitar.* Pacific, MO: Mel Bay, 1994. Solo, duet, trio, or quartet.

Schmid, Will. *The Chord Strummer.* Milwaukee: Hal Leonard Corporation, 1982.

———. *Contemporary Class Guitar,* Book 1. Milwaukee: Hal Leonard Corporation, 1982.

———. *Hal Leonard Guitar Method,* Book 1. Milwaukee: Hal Leonard Corporation, 1995.

———. *Rock Trax-1.* Milwaukee: Hal Leonard Corporation, 1985. Book and recording.

*———. *A Tribute to Woody Guthrie & Leadbelly.* Reston, VA: Music Educators National Conference, 1991. Student text and teacher's guide.

Share the Music, Grades K–8. New York: Macmillan/McGraw-Hill, 1995.

Snyder, Jerry. *Guitar Today,* Book 1. Van Nuys, CA: Alfred Publishing Company, 1982.

Stang, Aaron. *Guitar Rock Shop,* Book 1. Belwin's 21st-Century Guitar Library. Miami: CPP Belwin/Warner Bros. Publications, 1994.

Welch, Leo, and Nancy Marsters. *H.O.T. Hands-On Training: Second-Year Guitar.* Tallahassee, FL: Class Guitar Resources, 1992.

World of Music, Grades K–8. Parsippany, NJ: Silver Burdett Ginn, 1991.

Recordings Referenced in This Text

Burnin'. Bob Marley and the Wailers. Tuff Gong/Island 422-846200.

Caribbean Island Music. Elektra/Nonesuch 72047.

Dookie. Green Day. Reprise Records 945529-2.

Dowland, John. *Ayers and Lute Lessons.* Countertenor and period-instrument consort. Musique d'Abord/Harmonia Mundi HMA CD-1901076.

Duke Ellington: The Blanton-Webster Band. Various artists. RCA CD-5659-2-RB.

Flamenco! Pepe Romero. Mercury Living Presence CD-434 361-2.

*Folkways: A Vision Shared. Various artists. Columbia 44034.

*Folkways: The Original Vision. Woody Guthrie and Leadbelly. Smithsonian/Folkways SF-40001.

God Shuffled His Feet. Crash Test Dummies. Arista Records 74321-16531-2.

The Guitar Player Presents: Legends of Guitar. Rhino R270563.

Legend. Bob Marley and the Wailers. Tuff Gong/Island 42-846210.

Mas Canciones. Linda Ronstadt. Elektra 61239-2.

Music of the Chinese Pi'Pa. Nonesuch 702085-2.

*Music Resources for Multicultural Perspectives, 2d ed. Various artists. Music Educators National Conference 3017.

Oh, Happy Day. The Edwin Hawkins Singers. BMG Special Records 7243-8-56442-2-1.

Rocky Mountain High. John Denver. RCA 5190-2-R.

Roots of Reggae: Rock Steady. Rhino CD 72439.

Roots of Reggae: Ska. Rhino CD 72438.

Schubert, Franz. *An die Musik.* Bryn Terfel. Deutsche Grammophon CD-445 294-2.

Simon and Garfunkel's Greatest Hits. Columbia Records CK-31350.

Bessie Smith: The Complete Recordings, vol. 4. Columbia C2K 52838.

The Smithsonian Collection of Classic Jazz, vol. 3. Smithsonian Collection of Classic Jazz RD 033-3.

The Weavers' Greatest Hits. Vanguard Twofer VCD-15/16.

Other Resources Referenced in This Text

Bach Chorale Standard MIDI Files. Pacific, MO: Mel Bay. IBM, 95050IMD; Macintosh, 95050MMD.

*Folkways: A Vision Shared. New York: CBS Music Video Enterprises, 1988. Videocassette.

*Music Educators Journal. Periodical. Reston, VA: Music Educators National Conference.

*Teaching Music. Periodical. Reston, VA: Music Educators National Conference.

Additional Resources

Aebersold, Jamey. *Jazz: How to Play and Improvise.* Vol. 1 of *A New Approach to Jazz Improvisation.* Jamey Aebersold Jazz, PO Box 1244C, New Albany, IN 47151.

————. *Nothin' but Blues.* Vol. 2 of *A New Approach to Jazz Improvisation.* Jamey Aebersold Jazz, PO Box 1244C, New Albany, IN 47151.

Anderson, William M., and Joy E. Lawrence. *Integrating Music into the Classroom,* 4th ed. Belmont, CA: Wadsworth Publishing, 1998.

Anderton, Craig. *Multieffects for Musicians.* New York: Amsco Music, 1995.

Bacon, Tony, and Paul Day. *Ultimate Guitar Book.* New York: Alfred A. Knopf/Random House, 1997.

Bay, Mel. *Fun with Folk Songs.* Pacific, MO: Mel Bay Publications, 1963.

————. *Mel Bay's Complete Method for Modern Guitar.* Pacific, MO: Mel Bay Publications, 1980.

Bosman, Lance. *Harmony for Guitar.* New York: Music Sales/Carl Fischer, 1991.

Brooks, Tilford. *America's Black Musical Heritage.* Old Tappan, NJ: Prentice-Hall, 1984.

Burnett, Michael. *Jamaican Music.* New York: Oxford University Press, 1985.

Celentano, Dave. *The Art of Transcribing for Guitar.* Milwaukee: Centerstream/Hal Leonard Corporation, 1991. Book and recording.

Coffman, Don, John Webb, and Cathy Ellis. *The Advancing Jazz-Pop-Rock Guitarist.* Miami: Ellis Family Music, 1992–95.

Coker, Jerry. *Improvising Jazz.* New York: Touchstone, Simon & Schuster, 1986.

d'Auberge, Alfred, and Morton Manus. *Alfred's Basic Guitar Method,* Book 1, 3d ed. Van Nuys, CA: Alfred Publishing Company, 1990.

Davis, Stephen. *Reggae Bloodlines.* 1977. Reprint, New York: Da Capo Press, 1992.

Delaunay, Charles. *Django Reinhardt.* Milwaukee: Hal Leonard Corporation, 1961.

Gonzalez, Rene. *The Advancing Classical Guitarist,* rev. ed. Miami: Ellis Family Music, 1995.

Guitar Player Magazine editors. *Basic Guitar,* rev. ed. Milwaukee: GPI Publications/Hal Leonard Corporation, 1988.

Gustafson, Grant. *The Art of Guitar: Beginning Class Method.* San Diego: Neil A. Kjos Music Company, 1997.

Keil, Charles. *Urban Blues.* Chicago, IL: University of Chicago Press, 1968.

Leavitt, William G. *Classical Studies for Pick-Style Guitar: Solos and Duets.* 1968. Reprint, Milwaukee: Hal Leonard Corporation, 1986.

———. *A Modern Method for Guitar,* 3 vols. Milwaukee: Berklee/Hal Leonard Corporation, 1966. Books and recordings.

Marsters, Nancy. *H.O.T. Hands-On Training First-Year Guitar.* Tallahassee, FL: Class Guitar Resources, 1991. Book, teacher manual, and examination forms.

Marsters, Nancy, and Dawn Wooderson. *Guitar Ensembles,* beginning level. Tallahassee, FL: Class Guitar Resources, 1997.

McGuire, Edward. *Guitar Fingerboard Harmony.* Pacific, MO: Mel Bay Publications, 1976.

Megill, Donald D., and Richard S. Demory. *Introduction to Jazz History,* 4th ed. Old Tappan, NJ: Prentice-Hall/Simon & Schuster, 1994.

Noad, Frederic. *Solo Guitar Playing,* Book 1, 3d ed. Old Tappan, NJ: Schirmer/Simon & Schuster, 1994.

Roberts, John Storm. *Black Music of Two Worlds.* 1972. Reprint, Tivoli, NY: Original Music, 1982. Book and recording.

———. *The Latin Tinge,* 2d ed. New York: Oxford University Press, forthcoming.

Ross, Michael. *Getting Great Guitar Sounds.* Milwaukee: Hal Leonard Corporation, 1988.

Schmid, Will. *Beginning Guitar Superbook.* Milwaukee: Hal Leonard Corporation, 1995.

Shearer, Aaron. *Guitar Note Speller.* Miami: CPP Belwin/Warner Bros. Publications, 1985.

———. *Learning the Classic Guitar,* three parts. Pacific, MO: Mel Bay Publications, 1990. Books and recordings.

Somerville, L., and T. Pells. *Learn to Play Guitar.* Usborn Series. Tulsa, OK: EDC Publishing, 1988.

Stang, Aaron. *Guitar Method,* 3 books. Belwin's 21st-Century Guitar Library. Miami: CPP Belwin/Warner Bros. Publications, 1993–96.

Standing, Chris. *The Essential Studio Guitarist.* Milwaukee: Hal Leonard Corporation, 1994.

Stimpson, Michael. *Guitar: A Guide for Students and Teachers.* New York: Oxford University Press, 1988.

Summerfield, Maurice J. *Jazz Guitar: Its Evolution and Its Players,* 4th ed. Milwaukee: Hal Leonard Corporation, forthcoming.

Tedesco, Tommy. *Confessions of a Guitar Player.* Milwaukee: Centerstream/Hal Leonard Corporation, 1993.

Titon, Jeff Todd. *Early Downhome Blues,* 2d ed. Champaign, IL: University of Illinois Press, 1991.

Wilkes, Steve, Steve Defuria, and Joe Scacciaferro. *The Art of Digital Drumming.* Milwaukee: Ferro Technology/Hal Leonard Corporation, 1989. Book and recording.

*Available from MENC.

MENC Resources on Music and Arts Education Standards

Aiming for Excellence: The Impact of the Standards Movement on Music Education. 1996. #1012.

Implementing the Arts Education Standards. Set of five brochures: "What School Boards Can Do," "What School Administrators Can Do," "What State Education Agencies Can Do," "What Parents Can Do," "What the Arts Community Can Do." 1994. #4022. Each brochure is also available in packs of 20.

Music for a Sound Education: A Tool Kit for Implementing the Standards. 1994. #1600.

National Standards for Arts Education: What Every Young American Should Know and Be Able to Do in the Arts. 1994. #1605.

Opportunity-to-Learn Standards for Music Instruction: Grades PreK–12. 1994. #1619.

Performance Standards for Music: Strategies and Benchmarks for Assessing Progress Toward the National Standards, Grades PreK–12. 1996. #1633.

Perspectives on Implementation: Arts Education Standards for America's Students. 1994. #1622.

"Prekindergarten Music Education Standards" (brochure). 1995. #4015 (set of 10).

The School Music Program—A New Vision: The K–12 National Standards, PreK Standards, and What They Mean to Music Educators. 1994. #1618.

"Teacher Education in the Arts Disciplines: Issues Raised by the National Standards for Arts Education." 1996. #1609.

Teaching Examples: Ideas for Music Educators. 1994. #1620.

The Vision for Arts Education in the 21st Century. 1994. #1617.

MENC's *Strategies for Teaching* Series

Strategies for Teaching Prekindergarten Music, compiled and edited by Wendy L. Sims. #1644.

Strategies for Teaching K–4 General Music, compiled and edited by Sandra L. Stauffer and Jennifer Davidson. #1645.

Strategies for Teaching Middle-Level General Music, compiled and edited by June M. Hinckley and Suzanne M. Shull. #1646.

Strategies for Teaching High School General Music, compiled and edited by Keith P. Thompson and Gloria J. Kiester. #1647.

Strategies for Teaching Elementary and Middle-Level Chorus, compiled and edited by Ann Roberts Small and Judy K. Bowers. #1648.

Strategies for Teaching High School Chorus, compiled and edited by Randal Swiggum. #1649.

Strategies for Teaching Strings and Orchestra, compiled and edited by Dorothy A. Straub, Louis S. Bergonzi, and Anne C. Witt. #1652.

Strategies for Teaching Middle-Level and High School Keyboard, compiled and edited by Martha F. Hilley and Tommie Pardue. #1655.

Strategies for Teaching Beginning and Intermediate Band, compiled and edited by Edward J. Kvet and Janet M. Tweed. #1650.

Strategies for Teaching High School Band, compiled and edited by Edward J. Kvet and John E. Williamson. #1651.

Strategies for Teaching Specialized Ensembles, compiled and edited by Robert A. Cutietta. #1653.

Strategies for Teaching Middle-Level and High School Guitar, compiled and edited by William E. Purse, James L. Jordan, and Nancy Marsters. #1654.

Strategies for Teaching: Guide for Music Methods Classes, compiled and edited by Louis O. Hall with Nancy R. Boone, John Grashel, and Rosemary C. Watkins. #1656.

For more information on these and other MENC publications, write to or call MENC Publications Sales, 1806 Robert Fulton Drive, Reston, VA 20191-4348; 800-828-0229.

2712